LIFE'S
TRAGEDIES
God's Grace

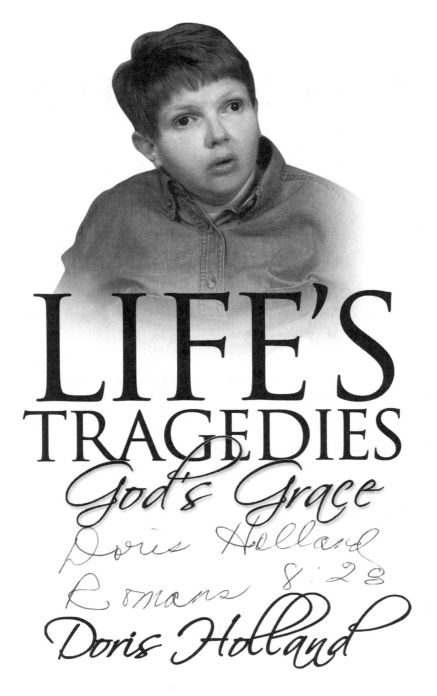

LIFE'S
TRAGEDIES
God's Grace

Doris Holland

Romans 8:28

Doris Holland

Author's
PUBLISHER
The New Generation of Publishing

LIFE'S TRAGEDIES
God's Grace

By Doris Holland
©2011 Doris Holland. All rights reserved.

ISBN: 978-0-9817009-3-9 Paperback

Published by:

 Author's PUBLISHER
The New Generation of Publishing

14805 Forest Road, Suite 106
Forest, VA 24551
www.AuthorsPublisher.com

Cover Wrap Design by:
Megan Johnson
www.Johnson2Design.com

Interior Design by:
Heather Kirk
www.GraphicsForSuccess.com

Dedicated to Rudy, Angie, Steve, Rylee, and Jon Patrick.
You bring great joy to my life.

In memory of Paul Rudolph Holland, II, our precious son.
You brought intelligence, wit, strength of character,
and just great fun to our family.
You represented Christ in a way that
would draw all men to Him.

ACKNOWLEDGMENTS

I am most grateful to Rudy, Angie, and Steve for their reflections, suggestions, and encouragement as I penned our family's story. Their prayerful support was essential when I struggled with the emotional parts of the book.

Nancy James, Editor, guided me through the finishing touches to make a clear and concise chronicle of our life's story.

Authors Publisher, Publisher, assisted in making this book a reality so we can share the story of God's grace in its many facets.

My heartfelt thanks to Monroe Roark, Betty Sue McNeil, and Millie Johnson for their technical assistance.

Michele Quick Photography did an outstanding job with our family picture.

All of the above helped me share our journey to be victors and not victims by the grace of God.

CONTENTS

FOREWORD
BY JONATHAN FALWELL
Pastor of Thomas Road Baptist Church, Lynchburg, VA

*G*race is defined as the free and unmerited favor of God. One of the greatest displays of God's grace is found in the gripping story of the Holland family. I have known the Holland family since I was a young child, and through these many years, I have witnessed great heartache and great victory in their lives as a result of their faith in the Giver of grace.

Through the words of these pages, you will take a journey that will, at times, lift the heart and, at times, bring tears to your eyes. You will witness firsthand, through the written word, how God always provides the grace that is needed to get us through each day.

In 2 Corinthians 3:5, Paul writes, *"Not that we are sufficient of ourselves to think of anything as being from ourselves, but our sufficiency is from God."* The Holland family has lived this verse out in daily life for many years. They know God is the Source of their strength and the Giver of grace in their lives. And, as a result, God has used them greatly.

I am certain that you will finish this book with a greater under-standing and appreciation of God's great love for you. And, I know you will be encouraged and strengthened in your walk with Christ. *Life's Tragedies God's Grace* is what God has done to this point, and grace for the rest of the journey is what you can depend on for the future. This book will help you see that the grace you need comes directly from the heart of God.

INTRODUCTION

*I*n 1991 my wife, Doris Holland, wrote a book, *Grace Thus Far*. That book was about the struggles of our family with a child who had a brain tumor that left him physically and mentally challenged. God's grace had seen us through and enabled us to continue in ministry and enjoy our lives.

This book, *Life's Tragedies God's Grace*, is the *Grace Thus Far* story and beyond. It shares the continuing growth of our family through a diversity of physical, emotional and spiritual challenges. Paul, our son, died in April, 2004. The trauma of the loss of a child, though not unexpected due to Paul's circumstances, is beyond comprehension to those who have never experienced this type of loss. Our entire family still grieves over the loss of Paul. However, "God's grace is sufficient," and our faith continues to increase. This book exposes the raw emotions of loss and hurt that can be used as a faith builder, not a detriment to our faith.

If the story stopped here, it would be enough; yet, God was still proving Himself to our family. As you read the book you will see our battles continue with the illness of our son-in-law. We still deal with this disease which demands more grace and challenges our faith. The illness of our son-in-law led him into an addiction to prescription drugs — another demand for grace and another challenge of our faith. Still, our family serves the God we love and trust.

The physical and emotional results of these battles are also presented — the anxiety and depression — again the need for more grace and a challenge of faith.

It is the prayer of the Holland and Donohoe families that this volume will reassure you of God's grace and will deepen your faith just as this journey has for our family.

Rudy Holland

1 Corinthians 10:13

CHAPTER 1
Birthday

As the rising sun first shone through our bedroom window, we sensed excitement in the air. Drowsiness gave way to the realization of the date: September 28, 1979. It was our daughter Angie's ninth birthday.

We had anticipated this special day and made plans for a cookout and "sleepover" for some of her girlfriends. How could I know this day would launch us on a journey that would alter our lives forever?

The children didn't need to be called twice to get ready for school. Rudy and I rushed around in usual preparation for our jobs as pastor and Christian school secretary, which kept us close each day to Angie and our seven-year-old Paul.

My busy day was interrupted by a phone call from the optometrist's office about an appointment to have Paul's eyes checked. Because of a scheduling conflict, they asked if we could come in that afternoon. I hesitated, thinking about Angie's party, but Rudy assured me he could watch the girls until Paul and I got home.

We had suspected Paul might need glasses because he could not read at the same level as he had the previous year. "He has started reversing his letters," his teacher said although he had overcome this problem in first grade.

When the bell rang at three o'clock to end the school day, Angie and Paul bounded into my office. We all loved Friday afternoon, with another week of school behind us and the weekend ahead to do fun things together.

I was needlessly concerned that Paul might be upset about the eye appointment. He was actually excited at the prospect of getting glasses. "Now all those yucky girls won't bother me," he said. I never ceased to be amazed at this child's ability to make an adventure out of a problem.

The optometrist gave Paul a thorough examination and answered all of his many questions, such as, "How does this machine work?" "Why does it make me see better?"

Near the end of the exam, I noticed the doctor kept shining a light in Paul's eyes. With a concerned look on his face, he instructed the attendant to take Paul into another room to look at frames; adding, "Paul needs glasses to correct astigmatism."

Once we were alone, however, he asked a different question. "Have you noticed that Paul's eyes do not respond properly to light stimulus?" Paul's eyes were a deep brown like his father's. I had never noticed that they did not dilate properly. The optometrist felt Paul might have a condition known as "Adie's pupil," a reflex problem where pupils simply do not open and close normally and said we should see an ophthalmologist, who is a medical doctor.

We knew Paul had problems with his vision but felt glasses could correct any deficit. I had no inkling that the cause of the condition might be far more serious than the visual symptoms indicated. After we chose just the right pair of glasses, we went home for the cookout and slumber party.

Later that night, as I lay in bed waiting for the giggles and squeals from the games and horror stories in the other room to subside, I thanked God for His many blessings upon my life. I reflected on my own childhood as the baby of a large family of four girls and two boys.

Like most families of that day, we had few luxuries. As a young couple, Mom and Dad worked hard just to buy the necessities for eight people. My wonderful Christian mother devoted all of her time and energy to her husband and children, and as a child I idolized her. Even though Dad was an alcoholic, Mom always stretched whatever money we had so she could feed and clothe us.

I often recalled how difficult it was to deal with my father's drinking problem. I loved him so much; but was confused and hurt by his erratic behavior when he drank.

Mom knew the importance of our Christian upbringing and always took us to Sunday school and church on Sunday, even though this did not always please Dad. We wanted him to come to church, but he always refused.

By my early teens, my Dad began to drink more heavily and stayed drunk many times into the weekdays. His escalated drinking and declining health made him miss work more and more frequently. I watched my Mom cry as she would call and lie that Dad was sick and could not come to work. She hated lying and for us to see her do so. I would feel sick in my gut as she almost seemed to cringe with shame. We children tried to act oblivious to these calls; we sensed her desperation for Daddy not to lose his job.

I could see the effects of trying to keep it all together were taking a terrible toll on my Mom. As the years wore on, she smiled less, sang less, cooked less; and the glimmer in her eyes began to fade. Fear became my companion in the dark night hours as my stability, my rock, my Mom no longer seemed invincible. In my mind, she was the glue that held it all together.

Up to this point in my life, God seemed vaguely abstract and distant to me. I thought maybe He just stayed at our church; it felt like He never came to our house. On Sunday morning when the preacher would talk about things I could not understand, the stories depicted in the stained glass windows made me feel close to Jesus. The scenes showed Him lovingly talking to little children, feeding a group of people, or healing a blind man. He looked so kind. However, all of their afforded comfort evaporated as we walked in the door at home. Dad would be angry and start an argument because we had gone to church again.

Out of a gnawing fear that things were getting worse, I began to pray frantically, "God if you really exist and care about me, will you please send someone to tell me how I can know you in a real way?" God was watching over this lonely, frightened teenage girl and heard my prayer. He led a young couple from Tennessee Temple College to start a church in our town. One day soon after I started praying, that young pastor's wife stopped by our house and invited me to church. I was awed on Sunday as that ministerial student preached that God loved me. He taught from the Bible how Jesus had died for our sins so we could be saved and know God in a personal way. It sounded too good to be true. Why would God care about me? I was too overwhelmed and confused by the simplicity of the Gospel story to respond to the invitation that Sunday morning. All afternoon I rehearsed in my mind again and again the story of God's love. When the pastor gave the invitation for salvation Sunday night, I could not resist God's call to my heart any longer.

I thanked God for loving me and drawing me as a 14-year-old teen unto Himself. That particular Sunday was on Christmas Eve which made His gift even more special to me. He really did exist and let me know Him not only as Savior but also as Lord. I cherished His promises of the blessed assurance that He would never leave me or forsake me.

As a mom myself, I appreciated my mother's faithfulness amidst extremely difficult circumstances. As much as she loved me, however, she could not always be my stability and my rock, neither was she invincible. Thank God I had met Jesus who could be that and more for me.

My thoughts frequently returned to those early days of growth as a Christian. As I stayed under the preaching and teaching of God's Word, I wanted to devote my life to bringing other people to know the love of Christ, but I didn't fully understand those longings.

One Sunday morning my pastor preached about giving one's life to full-time Christian service. I wondered how a woman could do that. My yearning was so strong that I had to talk to someone, so at the invitation I went forward and questioned my pastor. He explained that women could be missionaries or teachers and serve God in many other ways as well.

Though I had no idea how God could use a 16-year-old girl, I told Him and our church publicly that I would give my life to serve Him. I never dreamed that day of the diverse and sometimes difficult path my life would take.

Immediately I began to pray that God would provide for me to study at a Christian college. During my high school years Dad had become disabled due to his alcoholism, so with only the income from my mother's job there was no money for college. As a Christian teenager I had to ask God many times for guidance and special strength. How could I possibly pay for college? The money was an overwhelming concern for me at that time.

God began to build my faith in His provision as He provided babysitting jobs in addition to work at our local newspaper's office, and as a waitress at our dime store lunch counter. I enjoyed working and felt a sense of accomplishment. My little salary provided my lunch money and helped with other small expenses. These little baby steps of faith in my Heavenly Father's provision taught me to later trust Him for college funds. God met my need for jobs as a teen. His actions proved to be the foundational stones for me to trust Him as my needs became more substantial, and He never failed to fulfill His promises.

I had applied for a work scholarship at Tennessee Temple College, but they replied that none were available in the fall after my high school graduation. How could I ever fulfill God's call with my father disabled and no scholarship? After much agony and a deep sense of defeat, I prayed, "God, if you really want me to go to a Christian college and prepare to serve You, You will have to work this out."

Thinking about it again so many years later, I smiled as I considered the absolute miracle God worked in my life. I received a letter from Tennessee Temple. A work scholarship position had opened, and it was mine if I was willing to start in summer school. At the same time I received this wonderful news, my parents were informed that additional Social Security and veteran's benefits would allow them to help me financially. This was in the spring of 1965, and more than four decades later I remembered it as if it were yesterday.

Tennessee Temple met a great need in my life. It opened up a world of academic challenge, cultural opportunity and spiritual instruction to which I had never been exposed. Life seemed almost too good to be true.

I met a fine Christian young man, Rudy Holland, who had surrendered his life to preach the Gospel. As our relationship grew, I wondered if our marriage would allow me to find my place of full-time Christian service. Having heard many great missionaries tell of their work in Africa, Asia and other far-reaching places, I prayed and asked if a life on the mission field was what God wanted for me. I never felt God's call to be a missionary in another country although this would have been a noble call.

Rudy and I dated for a year and a half before we talked seriously about marriage. He had shared with me often how he was saved at the age of 18 and desired to serve the Lord. Raised in a Christian family in Lynchburg, Virginia, he attended Thomas Road Baptist Church but did not accept Christ until April of his senior year in high school.

He had worked at a restaurant for a year and a half and loved it. His plan was to study industrial management at a state college, but after being saved, he felt God directing him to attend Tennessee Temple instead. It was there, in January of his freshman year, that he answered the call to preach the Gospel. He changed from a general course curriculum to a major in Bible and minor in psychology.

For our Christian service assignments, we worked together in a youth camp on Saturday nights and with a church youth group each Sunday. Seeing high school kids accept Christ and experience major life changes made our sacrifices of free time on weekends worthwhile. Then, as now, this work brought joy and fulfillment.

Rudy's post-graduation plan was to attend seminary, but his pastor told him, "I think you should consider church planting." Rudy made quite a few trips to Virginia, evaluating different sites and seeking counsel from Christian leaders. We spent much time in prayer and felt this was God's plan for our lives.

When Rudy graduated from Tennessee Temple in the spring of 1970, we moved to Roanoke, Virginia, and started Berean Baptist Church in Salem, Virginia. Our daughter Angie was born September 28th of that year.

Our ministry grew fast, and we soon had enough people to start constructing a church building. In the summer of 1972 we moved into the sanctuary, complete with Sunday school facilities.

Our family life was happy and growing also. Rudy and I wanted a large family. On August 18, 1972, God gave us a beautiful baby boy, Paul, with blond hair and dark brown eyes.

In the ensuing years at the church we built children's and young people's departments, added a Christian school, a deaf ministry, a senior adult ministry, and bus routes to pick up people with no transportation to church. We worked with organizations for church planting and were instrumental in getting a bill passed in the state legislature to exempt church child care centers from licensure.

In retrospect, I can emphatically say that there were many struggles along the way. A growing church and Christian school ministry always faces difficulties. In addition, my precious mom and dad both died during those early church planting years. I adored my mom, and we had so wanted our children to know their grandparents and for them to be a part of Angie and Paul's lives. Why would God take my parents precisely at the time when they could truly enjoy freedom from raising six children? I learned to accept the difficult lesson that death was a part of life.

Lying in bed that night, my mind suddenly drifted back to the present. The giggles from the girls had stopped, and the only sound I heard was restful breathing in a house full of children after a long day of school and fun.

I ended my prayer and meditation by thanking God for all of the love, guidance and blessing He had bestowed upon that 16-year-old girl who had surrendered her life to full-time Christian service without really understanding what it would mean. I remember quite vividly asking God, "Make me a loving, compassionate Christian like my mom," with no idea of the valleys and trials God had allowed her to go through to become a vessel fit for His use.

As I fell asleep, it seemed as if He were asking me, "Are you really willing to surrender that much to My will?" I mumbled my answer, not knowing that on that very day I had begun a long, difficult journey where at various times I would question Him, praise Him, be angry at Him, cry out in agonizing prayer for help from Him, become bitter at Him, and love Him for His watch care over us. Prayerfully, through it all, I would come to know the truth of Romans 8:28. *"And we know that all things work together for good to them that love God, to them who are the called according to His purpose."*

CHAPTER 2
Dreaded Diagnosis

*P*aul and I kept our appointment with the ophthalmologist the next week. We waited and waited until we had read every children's book in the waiting room and played every quiet game we knew.

Finally they called us. To our pleasant surprise, a lady from our church was the doctor's assistant.

Paul jumped up in the chair for his examination and started his barrage of questions: "What does this machine do? How does it work?" Exceptionally bright and precocious, Paul was interested in everything and everyone around him.

The doctor examined him thoroughly and said, "Since I feel certain that Paul has an Adie's pupil, you need not do anything else at this time."

Paul and I went into the hall and started chatting with the assistant. She asked how Paul had been feeling, since he had previously been diagnosed as having juvenile migraine headaches.

"Aspirin controls them, but we will be so glad when he outgrows them," I replied. "We are going to have him checked by an endocrinologist because he tires easily. He also has been wetting his pants accidentally from time to time. We're afraid that juvenile diabetes might even be a possibility."

The doctor came over and asked to speak to me again. I didn't know it, but he had heard our entire conversation.

"What I heard, along with Paul's vision problems, makes me feel that you need to see your pediatrician immediately," he said.

"Why?"

"There's no cause for worry. But there could be a connection between all of these symptoms."

That night Rudy and I tried to assure each other not to panic, even though in both of our hearts there was a growing fear that something serious might be wrong with Paul. As I prayed during my devotional time, I thanked God for this child of the love Rudy and I shared. I realized that if we could have taken a catalog and selected the traits we would wish for in a little boy, Paul had them all.

Angie was always a petite child. "What she lacks in size, she makes up for in will," we often joked. I often thought as I read books about strong-willed children that if there were a contest for such a trait, Angie would win hands down. It astonished us to see such a tiny two-year-old put her hands on her hips and say no to everything even when she meant yes. It took years of loving patience, guidance and discipline to direct all of that determination into a beautiful young woman who loves and honors our Lord. Her God-given will of iron makes her a great leader, and her heart of gold makes her a willing servant.

When Paul was born I prayed, "God, please do not give me another child with a will of iron." To our surprise and delight, this child understood the meaning of such words as "Stop," "No," and "Mommy doesn't want you to do that." He was always so outgoing and bright that life was a constant source of excitement for him.

Paul and Angie fussed and fought like any siblings, but she was fiercely protective of him with older children. I often prayed, "Father, we gave Paul to you even while he was still in my womb. Take him and use him for your glory." Rudy and I sometimes thought that might mean God would send Paul to a faraway country some day, and we might not see him very often.

We always shared Bible stories with our children at night when we put them to bed and, of course, they attended Sunday school regularly. My kids always teased me that they had a nine-month head start because

I went to church all through my pregnancies. Even so, I was surprised one day when six-year-old Paul came into the kitchen and said he wanted to talk to me.

"What is it, Paul?" I asked. "I'm making dinner."

"Turn off the stove and come to my bedroom," he said.

After we sat down he said, "Mom, I just asked Jesus to come into my heart."

I was delighted, but because of his age I wanted to make certain he understood what he had done. I took the Bible and we went over verses about God's love for us and how Jesus came so we could have eternal life.

"I know that, Mom," he said, "and I just asked Jesus to come into my heart."

I called his father at the church and told him what happened. "Don't tell Paul you called me," Rudy said. "Let's see what he says when I get home."

That night at dinner Paul said, "Dad, I got saved today." We rejoiced with him but were still anxious to be sure he understood.

We were surprised again the following Sunday when Paul came forward during the invitation and told our assistant pastor he had been saved and wanted to join the church. After a few more questions and instructions, we felt sure that he was ready to follow the Lord in believer's baptism.

Not many months after this, Paul began to express a desire to be a preacher like his dad. I smiled at the way he expressed it.

One Sunday one of the men in our church asked Paul, "What do you want to be when you get big?"

"Well, I am going to be a preacher," he replied without hesitation.

"Where will you preach?"

"Here at Berean."

"But where will your dad preach?"

"Oh, he'll be dead by then."

The man chuckled and asked, "Where will you get your sermons?"

"That's no problem," said Paul. "Dad has hundreds of them!"

After Paul's diagnosis, I wondered how a serious illness might affect his ability to study and prepare to preach.

The pediatrician conducted a thorough examination, including blood work, and said that he found nothing to indicate a serious problem like diabetes. When he sensed that we were not completely reassured, he referred us to a neurologist. The appointment clerk informed us that because of a cancellation we would be able to come in the very next day.

As we rode in the car to that appointment, Paul seemed concerned about something. I thought he might be dreading yet another doctor's appointment, so I asked him what was bothering him.

"When my teacher measured all the kids today, I was the shortest boy," he said. "Last year I was one of the tallest boys; how can I be the shortest one this year?"

I agreed that this was strange, but I was not overly alarmed. I did, however, make a mental note to share this with the neurologist.

The doctor took Paul into another room to administer some tests along with a complete neurological exam. He returned and explained that he could find nothing that overly concerned him except that Paul was a little behind on some motor skills. He asked the cause of my concern that something was seriously wrong.

"Paul has so many different problems that I wondered if they all might be related," I said, telling him of the juvenile migraine headaches, vision problems, fatigue, intolerance for heat, pants-wetting, and now Paul's concern that everyone was growing faster than he was.

As the expression on the doctor's face grew more and more concerned, I felt as though someone were squeezing my chest. I could not seem to get enough air into my lungs.

"We need to do some neurological tests, including an EEG and CAT scan, to rule out any possibility of a pituitary lesion," the doctor suggested. "Many of these problems could be related to a low-functioning pituitary."

I was too numb to ask more questions, but as the nurse scheduled the time for the EEG I realized I didn't really know what a pituitary lesion was. So I asked her.

"A brain tumor," she replied.

An icy numbness came over me. I choked out a whispered "thank you" as she handed me the appointment card and we left. Once again, I felt as if there was not enough air in my lungs.

Keeping my promise to Paul, I took him to Arby's for lunch even though I knew I couldn't swallow any food. I forced myself to sit quietly while he ate. I wanted to cry out to everyone in the restaurant, "How can you sit there and eat, laugh and talk, when my son may have a brain tumor?" I felt surreal as if I were not a part of the surroundings.

As I drove back to school trying to act normal, my mind was swirling; how could I tell Rudy that our precious little boy might have a brain tumor? But later that day, when I poured out my worst fears to him, he assured me, "No matter what's ahead, we can handle it with God's help."

The next few days of sheer agony seemed to drag on forever.

When we got to the hospital that day, we were all relieved to note that another lady from our church would assist with Paul's CAT scan. As they called his name, all three of us tried to act brave but each of us had tears streaming down our faces as Paul was led away. Even though Paul tried to act big-boy tough, Rudy and I knew he was very scared about having the dye put in his veins for the CAT scan.

When we returned for the EEG appointment, it was hard for Paul to sit still long enough to have all the electrodes glued to his head, but he was a little trooper and didn't even cry. We tried to make him understand everything that would be happening to him during all the tests. Later that morning Rudy and I went to get something to drink and saw the assistant coming out of another room. When she saw us, she flashed an agonized look and backed into the same room.

Rudy and I froze right there in the hall, knowing by her expression that something was dreadfully wrong. Another lady brought Paul out, and although we had so many questions she told us we would have to wait for a call from the neurologist.

At times like this one of the hardest things to do is carry on with one's normal activities. Rudy had to check his messages at the church and pick up Angie from school, so he suggested Paul and I go home and try to get some rest.

As I lay on the bed at home beside Paul, he quickly dozed off. Hot tears trickled down the sides of my face as I gently played with his hair, begging God for a good report from the doctor. The longer I lay there the more upset I became.

I got up to start dinner while straining hard to hear every car on our street, so I could rush out and hear what Rudy had to say as soon as he got home. But when I recognized the sound of our car I couldn't seem to make my feet move.

Neither of us could speak when Rudy came in the front door. I knew that if the report had been good he would have called earlier or come rushing in with the news. Thankfully, our associate pastor and his wife had also come to take Angie and Paul out for ice cream so Rudy and I could talk. I knew I couldn't break down in front of the kids so I numbly got them freshened up to go.

After they left, Rudy and I sat down in the living room and he spoke the words I had so greatly dreaded: "Brain tumor." When you are dealing with a serious illness or the impending death of someone in your family, you always hope that it might not be true until you hear the words spoken aloud.

The neurologist had called Rudy at about 3:15 p.m. As God would have it, Rudy was not alone; he was meeting with a church trustee and our assistant pastor. After the doctor gave the report, Rudy looked across his desk and said for the first time, "Paul has a brain tumor."

"I don't know what to say," said the church trustee with tears in his eyes. "You know more of the promises of God than I do."

"What are you going to tell Doris?" the assistant pastor asked.

Rudy said he would go home immediately and give me the report. He did not want to do it over the phone or in front of the children, so the assistant pastor said that he and his wife would take Paul and Angie out for a few hours.

During this time the school day had ended, and Angie was waiting outside for her dad to take her home. As the two men left, Rudy called Angie in and asked her to come over to his desk. He put his arms around her and told her he had a little bit of bad news, but everything would be OK. He told her about the brain tumor and that Paul must have surgery.

Even though Rudy was dying inside, he wanted to reassure Angie and answer all of her questions. Angie didn't have any questions, so Rudy told her that later she could go out for ice cream with Paul.

Back in our living room, Rudy explained the diagnosis and procedures to me. "Paul must have extensive surgery to remove the tumor as soon as they can assemble the necessary team for this type of operation."

I had so many questions. Would he suffer? Would he have any residual problems as a result of the surgery? Was there any other way to treat the tumor?

Finally we both got on our knees, weeping and asking God to watch over Paul and give us the strength to face all that lay ahead. As Rudy prayed, he asked God to let us live as a testimony to our church people of what he had preached to them regarding the faithfulness of God in the hour of trouble.

When we finished praying, we realized that nightfall had come and we had not turned the lights on. Just when we needed comfort, the Lord sent the church trustee and his wife to pray with us and assure us that our church members were already praying. They were calling Christians all over the nation to pray. The outpouring of love and support for us during the next few weeks was phenomenal.

CHAPTER 3

Surgery

Two of my sisters and my niece came to be with us at home while we waited for the surgery. Each day was like an eternity as Paul's condition deteriorated rapidly. His headaches were almost constant and his right eyelid began to droop. Angie's birthday, only two and a half weeks earlier, seemed like ages ago.

People were so eager to help. We received beautiful notes and cards, and many friends called the church and our home to express their love and concern while offering to help in any way possible.

Some good intentions proved very stressful to us. People we hardly knew called to suggest alternative medical treatment for Paul, such as going to other countries for diets or procedures not available in the United States. Finally we talked to Paul's neurologist and he assured us that they were aware of all advances in medical technology and would only recommend the best possible treatment for Paul.

The surgical team was finally assembled and a date was set: October 16, 1979.

After we checked into the hospital, the neurosurgeon stopped by and talked with us about Paul's surgery. He explained several frightening possibilities, such as ongoing problems with vision and motor skills as a result of surgery. Paul could even die during the procedure.

I know informing families of all possible dangers is necessary, but that didn't make it any easier. The hot tears flowed, and my body shook as we tried to grasp all that was said.

"They will come soon and shave Paul's head in preparation for the surgery," said the neurosurgeon. Maybe no one except a mother could understand how much I did not want them to cut off his beautiful blond hair. Once that happened, the entire experience would become even more real for me.

The surgeon sensed my dread and said that they would wait and shave Paul's head in the morning just before the operation. Then the endocrinologist came in and tried to prepare us for the insatiable thirst Paul would have after surgery as a result of trauma to the pituitary gland.

Soon it was time to settle Paul for the night. Rudy and I sat there into the wee hours praying for God to take care of our little boy. Paul became very restless and thirsty (he was not allowed to drink anything after midnight), so he and Rudy walked the halls until he got tired and could sleep for a few more minutes.

Morning finally came and it was time for the pre-op shots. Paul tried so hard to be brave but he cried each time a needle punctured his skin. When that was completed, the staff came with a gurney to take him away.

We were allowed to walk as far as the elevator with him. I distinctly remember the snap of the doors as they closed. We had to put our son's life in someone else's hands. Would Paul live through the surgery? If so, what permanent damage would he have?

Rudy's family, my family, and nearly 20 friends stayed with us throughout the day. It is a strange feeling to sit and talk with people and really not grasp what is being said. All I could think about was Paul lying in that operating room.

As the afternoon drew to a close, our surgeon finally appeared and gave his report. He had been able to get most of the tumor, but he thought Paul's optic nerve had suffered some damage.

We quickly thanked all of our friends and rushed to neuro-intensive care. We were not at all ready for what we saw.

Paul's head was bandaged, and there were tubes running everywhere. He was connected to machines monitoring his heart and respirations, yet when we walked into the room his eyes popped open. He wanted to know where his drink of water was that his dad had promised him the night before when they walked the halls.

We were thrilled beyond words to see his intellect and vision intact.

The difficult part was that we could only give him small bites of ice and his thirst grew worse and worse. Soon he was crying out in anguish for water, but it was still too soon after the surgery for him to have any. Because the tumor and surgery had damaged his pituitary gland, the hormone that works in the kidneys needed to make the body reabsorb water was not being produced. We could not make him understand this; therefore, he begged constantly for water.

Hours later the doctor finally gave the order that Paul could have his anti-diuretic hormone and then something to drink. He drank and drank until he vomited all over the sheets but still received no relief until the hormone took effect.

When the hormone started to work, he finally fell asleep. We thanked God the worst was over.

Unknown to us at the time, Angie had cried all day at school. She had seen her brother get increasingly worse during the week and could sense the stress as our family and church members came to visit. As everyone expressed their concern for Paul she realized that it was more than just a simple operation to make his headaches better.

That morning when her class had prayer time, all of her bottled-up fears broke loose into near hysteria. We had thought she would be better off at school and had not sensed how she felt so alone and not a part of what was going on with Paul. In retrospect, we know she would have been much better off at the hospital with us. Children are so much more aware of what is happening than we as parents think, and our trying to protect her had only made her fears worse.

Experience on a pediatric floor in the hospital proved to be a real shock for me. We realized that families react very differently to sickness in their children.

Rudy and I were fortunate that at least one of us could stay with Paul around the clock so he would not be afraid of being left alone. We saw children as young as three years old who were alone. One little girl in particular cried and screamed almost all the time. We learned that she was from a bad home situation and was left at the hospital by herself most of the time.

Angie would go over and read to her whenever she visited Paul. One night as Rudy and Angie were leaving the hospital, Rudy asked Paul, "Is there anything I can bring you?"

"Can you buy that little girl a doll and bring it to her?" Paul asked, thinking that such a gift might help her not to feel so alone.

The next day Paul and Angie took the doll over to the little girl's room and told her it would be her special friend when she was alone and afraid. We never dreamed that several years later Rudy would be instrumental in helping one of our church families provide a permanent home for that little girl's baby sister.

After about ten days Paul was up and about, ready to go home. His post-operative exam revealed that he had lost his peripheral vision in both eyes and was legally blind in his right eye.

Soon, however, he was able to go back to school. I was concerned about how the other children would react to Paul when they saw such a big scar and no hair on his head. I knew Angie was fiercely protective of her little brother, but I was not aware that before Paul returned to school she had marched into his classroom with her hands on her hips and said, "If anyone makes fun of Paul, they will have to deal with me." I still wonder how she thought anyone as tiny as she was could deal with anyone.

Paul had me buy him a lollipop, and when he went back to school he announced that he was Kojak. Children have their own unique outlook on life, and the school children thought Paul was quite the hero to have been in the hospital, and to have gone through surgery. It was quite cool to flash a scar from ear to ear.

Our neurosurgeon's prognosis for Paul was better than we had hoped. He would always have his visual problems and be on total hormonal replacement, yet we were so thankful he had not suffered any brain damage.

The neurosurgeon also felt that Paul's tumor would not return for 7 to 10 years, by which time laser technology should be advanced to the point that we could opt for laser surgery on the tumor without any further damage to his vision. We could not understand God's purpose in letting Paul have a brain tumor, but we were thankful He had returned our son to us.

Life indeed took on a more precious meaning because of this experience. The thought of possibly losing your child brings your priorities quickly into focus.

When Rudy and I started our family, our decision was for me to stay home with them, at least until they were in school. We have often joked about how poor we were in those days. A big night out on the town was a McDonald's hamburger on Sunday night after church.

Our children always brought such joy to us that anything we did with them was fun. By necessity, family outings were usually activities that cost almost no money, such as going to the park or just having friends over for a play date. Now each day was even more precious.

After Paul recuperated and was back in school, Rudy was invited to speak at a pastors' meeting in Richmond. Riding all alone on the trip to the conference, Rudy began to ask the Lord what God wanted him to learn from this traumatic experience in our family. As he drove down the road he jotted down five lessons he had learned. Little did he know those five statements would grow into a message God would use across the nation to encourage the hearts of hurting people.

CHAPTER 4
Surgery Again

We had a wonderful summer the next year until about the first week of August, when I sensed Paul once again was not feeling well. At first he exhibited just small symptoms, like not wanting to go out and play. A checkup by his endocrinologist showed nothing out of control with his hormones.

I grew more and more concerned as one symptom after another returned. One night when we had company at our house and were preparing to go to a church softball game, Paul came to me and said, "My head hurts so bad, and I feel sick to my stomach."

Fear gripped my heart as I called Rudy to come upstairs. "Is there any way Paul's tumor could be back?" I asked in near hysterics.

"We'll call Paul's physician," said Rudy with a comforting voice.

Paul's doctor felt sure he was not in any real danger, but he said he would be happy to see us in his office as soon as the nurse could give us an appointment. I finally pulled myself together so we could go the game, but an incredible fear gripped my heart.

In bed later that night, Rudy and I talked, prayed, and cried until the wee hours of the morning. What could be done for Paul if his tumor had already grown back? The laser surgery was not yet available. We tried to comfort each other but both of us felt that something terrible might be happening to Paul, and there might not be anything we could do for him. It is one thing to face a crisis when you feel there is something you can do to correct it or fix it, but it is a totally different fear when you think maybe you can do nothing to help.

Horrible dread hovered over our lives again until we could find out what was happening with Paul. While we waited for an appointment with the neurologist, the hospital called to say they had a cancellation that day for the CAT scan machine and they could work Paul in if we could bring him in that morning. Rudy came home and took Paul and me to the hospital. As we approached the building all of our old familiar dreads and fears rushed over us. "God, please don't let them come back with a bad report," I prayed.

We hated so much for Paul to have the dye put in his veins again, but he was so brave and tried not to cry. I remember thinking, "God, why couldn't I be the one to be sick? A child should not have to go through all this."

Rudy and I went outside to wait. Normally you can't find out the results of the test until the physician who ordered the CAT scan calls you later, so Rudy and I were surprised when the radiologist came out and asked to speak with us. We had met him the year before and found him to be a very caring and compassionate doctor.

As soon as he read the CAT scan, he saw that it was not good and immediately called Paul's neurologist to give him a report. He informed us that the neurologist wanted us to come over to his office and bring the film with us.

Many times a person's body goes into a state of shock when there is more trauma than the mind can deal with. For me, this was one of those times. I became so cold and felt numb as Paul's neurologist showed us the film revealing a large tumor. I looked at that mass of tissue that could kill our child and felt such hatred for this intruder in his little body. Somehow I wanted to reach into Paul's head and tear it out. It was an enemy I wanted to destroy.

But we were totally defenseless as the neurologist said, "I am not sure what we can do to help Paul. I will consult with his neurosurgeon and get back with you."

We somehow drove home. Rudy called family members and close friends with the news, and his parents came down to be with us. They had bought Paul a riding toy called a Green Machine for his upcoming birthday, and they wanted to bring it with them. Paul's grandfather felt that putting it together would give him and Rudy a way to pass the time.

When it was ready, they called Paul outside to take it for a spin. He was very excited as he rode it down the driveway. When he came back up to the house, he got off and grabbed his head.

"Daddy, my head hurts so bad," he said. "Can I go inside?"

I was on the phone with Paul's doctor, so his grandmother said she would go upstairs with him. When Paul lay down on his bed he said that he felt like he would vomit, so grandmother got him a receptacle and a wet washcloth for his forehead. Soon he started vomiting.

"Nanny, why does Jesus let my head hurt like this?" he asked his grandmother between bouts of vomiting.

"I don't know, honey," she replied. "But I do know God loves you."

As Rudy came upstairs to check on Paul, he heard his son singing "Jesus Loves Me" amid the gagging. Paul had the total faith of a child that, even though this bad thing was happening to him, God loved him and would watch over him.

Once again we had to outwardly maintain a normal existence while we waited for the treatment options from the doctors.

I remember asking the neurosurgeon at our next appointment what he could do to help Paul. I am sure it is a horrendous task for a doctor to help parents cope with the reality of a serious illness in their children. I guess he felt the only way he could make me grasp the severity of Paul's illness was by shocking me into reality.

"Doris," he said, "Paul has a disease that is going to kill him, and you have to accept this."

He went on to explain that they would perform surgery and put a pump into Paul's cysts that would allow them to aspirate the fluid from them when they filled up again. They would also put in shunts to help drain fluid off the brain, but they couldn't successfully take out Paul's tumor because it was attached to the brain stem and the carotid artery. Total removal was impossible.

It began to dawn on us that he was just talking about buying time. How do you accept the fact that your child is going to die? We somehow sat through the rest of the appointment as he told us the surgery date and finished explaining what they hoped to do at that time.

When we got in the car, for the first time I saw Rudy break down and sob. We were both devastated. How could we go through this? Why would the Lord ask this of us? We had surrendered our children to Him, but at that moment I felt like He was asking too much. I wanted my children to serve Him, but not in this way. "God, anything but please don't take my child!" I thought.

Angie and Paul were the most precious things in the world to us. "O God, we wanted these children so much," I prayed. "We've done everything in our power to be the best parents we could be. Have we done something wrong? Why? WHY?"

I am sure people drove past our car and wondered what was wrong, but we were totally oblivious to everything around us. We knew we had to get ourselves together somehow so we could pick up Angie and Paul and go home. After we got the kids settled that night, Rudy and I prayed and prayed, asking God to give us direction and strength.

The surgery date came around quickly. Once again we had a lot of people with us for support. We had let Angie come that morning to tell her brother goodbye as he went to surgery. Since we let her have a part in taking Paul to the hospital, Angie understood more clearly what was happening and handled this surgery much better than the first. She also thought that since the first surgery came out all right, everything would be fine after this one.

I tried to talk but was so nervous I could only walk back and forth. My skin felt as if it would crawl off my body. Everyone was so supportive. Rudy had to be strong for both of us; I don't know how I could have made it through without his strength.

After about eight hours, the surgeon came out and took Rudy and me aside to tell us the operation was complete.

"The tumor was very large," he said. "I removed as much as I could without jeopardizing Paul's life."

My heart went out to him as he stood there looking so exhausted. He looked so sad as he told us there was nothing else he could do for Paul.

We went downstairs quickly to see Paul, but we couldn't go in immediately. I remember that horrible feeling of someone crushing my chest and squeezing all the air out of my lungs as we sat and waited. Fear and anxiety was so strong that I felt like I would die.

Soon we saw Paul and were thankful that his mind and vision were intact. As we sat by his hospital bed, we knew we had to accept his illness and make his remaining time as good as it could be for him.

We desperately wanted to be sure we had tried everything possible to save Paul's life.

The next day Rudy began to call major medical centers all over the country to see if there was any treatment available that could help Paul. He talked with one of the physicians at the University of Virginia, and she suggested we contact the Boston Children's Hospital.

Rudy called, and they did have a relatively new radiation therapy treatment for Paul's particular tumor. They would consult with our physicians and let us know if they would accept him into the program.

We were torn. Was this the right thing to do for Paul? Were we grasping at straws? Yet we knew as parents we had to try everything possible. We talked with our local physicians and they felt it was an appropriate treatment. Representatives of Boston Children's Hospital called and said they would accept Paul into the program as soon as he could travel.

When a catastrophic illness hits a family, it brings with it many other problems.

While Paul was in the hospital, he received numerous gifts and cards almost every day. One particular day Rudy's parents brought a large box of very nice gifts and cards to Paul from Mr. Holland's department at work. We were deeply appreciative, and Paul was thrilled with the gifts.

Angie was only nine years old at the time and although she knew Paul was sick, she couldn't understand how sick he really was. All she knew was that he did not have to go to school, everyone catered to his every wish, and he got presents all the time. She began to make bad grades (she had always been a good student), complained constantly about a stomach ache and started misbehaving. We wondered what in the world was happening.

I sat her down for a talk. "Honey, what is wrong with you?" I asked. "Why are you not acting like yourself while your brother is so sick?"

"Paul isn't all that sick," she said as she started to cry. "He doesn't have to go to school and he gets all those nice presents."

In her little heart she felt no one cared about her because everyone talked about Paul all the time and brought him presents. Why didn't anyone like her?

Rudy had also uncovered these feelings in Angie. One morning as they rode to school she told her father, "Dad, I wish I had a brain tumor."

"Angie, why would you say something like that?"

"So I can get presents like Paul and not have to go to school."

Her dad did not reply, but he knew we had to do something to counteract those feelings of anger and jealousy in Angie's heart. We were so sorry we had not realized how alone and unloved she felt. One of us always tried to be at home with her, but she was being shuffled around a lot as we constantly were on the go to the doctor's office or the hospital, or on the phone trying to line up the trip to Boston.

One of the most difficult tasks during a catastrophic illness is to spread yourself around enough to meet the needs of all your children. Yet this is of colossal importance. We realized we had to improve our communication with Angie so she would better understand her brother's illness and how it affected our whole family. We told her everything that we felt she could deal with though we did not feel appropriate at the time to tell her Paul might die.

To help her get past these feelings of being left out, we wanted to find a definite visual sign of our concern for her that a child her age could relate to and understand. On special occasions over the years we had bought her dolls with costumes that represent the dress of other countries. They were not expensive, but she loved to display them in her room. One day while Paul and I were at the hospital, Rudy went out and bought her several of these dolls and put them in the trunk of the car. On days she felt really left out, he would slip out to the car and bring one in to her. I can remember seeing him put her on his lap and explain to her how important she was to us just before giving her the doll. Many times when I came home for a rest from the hospital I would see that she had placed the dolls in her room so she could see them as she fell asleep.

Another area of extreme duress was the constant financial pressure. Because of Paul's recent surgery and recuperation, plus the upcoming six-week stay in Boston and recuperation afterward, I had to take a leave of absence from my job until at least after the Christmas holidays. We had no idea how much we would have to pay toward the doctor and hospital bills. On top of that, how were we going to pay for plane tickets to Boston, a place to stay, food to eat, and transportation to and from the hospital?

We began to immediately see the hand of the Lord in meeting our needs. Our church set up a trust fund where people could contribute to help us with these expenses. Two families who visited our church came over for a snack after the service and, knowing of our special needs, put some money in Rudy's coat pocket as they left our home that night. Later we realized this was the exact amount we needed for airfare to Boston.

We still did not know how God would meet our every need, but we could see Him beginning already to supply each need.

CHAPTER 5
Our Final Hope

As our preparations for Boston began, we had many concerns. A top priority was to see that Angie had a place to stay where she could maintain her normal schedule as much as possible, feel secure within that family, and be able to enjoy staying for six weeks. We asked her which families she felt she would be comfortable with and then prayed for God to touch their hearts to volunteer to keep her.

One particular family we all felt very comfortable with approached us about caring for her. This was a tremendous answer to prayer as we knew she would have a difficult adjustment once we left for Boston. Six weeks is a long time to stay away from home when you are only ten years old.

Rudy and I had no idea where Paul and I would stay in Boston for the five weeks after he was released from the hospital. We had no friends or relatives in that area. This was especially disturbing for Rudy, who wondered how we could afford housing, food and transportation costs. He shared these concerns with a local pastor friend who said he knew a pastor in Boston and would contact him to see if his church could assist us.

As the time to get on that plane grew nearer, I approached our departure with both hope and apprehension. Would the radiation work? Where would we stay? Would Angie do OK? Despite my concerns, I knew this was our only hope.

We had been told that someone from the church in Boston would meet us when we arrived. Rudy, Paul and I felt alone as we walked though Logan International Airport when suddenly a beautiful lady stepped up and asked, "Are you the Holland's?" Tears came to my eyes as I knew God was watching over us and had sent this special person to meet us.

We loaded our luggage into her car and she asked if we minded riding with her to her office. She normally didn't volunteer for this kind of service because of the demands of her business, but when the pastor asked for someone to meet us she volunteered. "I'm still not sure why I did it," she said with a laugh.

As we rode across Boston she pointed out many interesting sites. I love history and soon began to relax as we began our first-ever visit to this historic city. We shared with her in more detail why were in Boston and asked if she knew where we could rent a room for the duration of Paul's treatment.

After a brief stop at her office, our host said she wanted us to meet her family. It was late afternoon by this time and after the introductions they invited us to go out for dinner. Here we were, on our first night in a strange city, having a meal with a wonderful family who was opening up their home to us. We felt God had given us a family away from home.

The grandmother was planning to move from the family home into an apartment right next door in a few days. Instead she insisted that Paul and I stay there rent-free, after Paul was released from the hospital. We did not know how to respond as we knew rent in that area was high (it was near Harvard University) and she could easily find a paying tenant. But they assured us that this was their desire. Not only that, they loaned us an automobile to use until we either rented a car or decided to use public transportation.

After dinner they took us to our motel near the hospital, as we had an early-morning appointment the next day. It is hard to describe the complete feeling of peace that flooded our minds and hearts as we saw God supply our every need from the moment we stepped off the plane.

The next few days proved to be a bit frightening. We met with one doctor after another as they monitored Paul's treatment. The list included a neurologist, endocrinologist, radiologist, ophthalmologist, and pediatricians. We also met a barrage of nurses and technicians who would assist with Paul's care.

We spent most of one day with the neurologist and radiologist as they explained exactly what they would do and what the side effects could be. Paul would actually receive the radiation treatments at Peter Bent Brigham Hospital, shuttling between there and Boston Children's each day while he was still hospitalized.

Paul's hair had just begun to grow back, and they had to shave it on the sides again to mark it for the radiation. I watched his little eyes grow with fear as they marked his head and gave us a tour of the radiation department. Of course, Rudy and I were equally afraid but we knew we had to appear calm and in control so we could provide the security he needed. All of the medical staff was so compassionate and concerned and all our questions were answered.

Paul had to stay in the hospital for the first few treatments. Once they started he began vomiting again and in general did not feel well. While he was awake, Rudy or I would read to him or take him to the game room. We tried to provide as much entertainment as he could handle, to help pass the time.

Soon Rudy had to leave us and go back to work and be near Angie. Paul did not feel well at all and slept much of the time. The day Rudy had to leave, I felt so alone.

In Boston Children's Hospital my eyes and heart were exposed to sights and sounds I never really knew existed — a world of very sick children. We met one child after another with a terminal disease, and I talked with parents who, like us, were doing everything possible to give their child the opportunity to live.

I grew up in a large family of healthy children. In fact, as a child I wondered why I could never be sick like the other children and miss school. I knew that children could be desperately sick but had never been around any terminally ill children before. My heart was wrenched with the pain of these children and their families. Seeing suffering children had a profound effect on me.

One especially painful experience took place in the room Paul shared with another little boy dying of a brain tumor. His mother, an older woman, told me how she and her husband had not been able to have a child for many years. They had prayed that God would give them just one son.

Her eyes beamed as she shared with me her joy at having a beautiful baby boy after many years of trying. She described her husband's joy in playing ball with his son. How they loved him!

Suddenly she stopped and said, "You are a pastor's wife. Tell me, why would God let my son die?"

Her words shot through me like a searing bolt of lightning. How could I answer her when I was asking God the same question?

I remember so clearly her pleading look as she waited for me to answer, and I had absolutely no power within myself to do that. I felt as if time had stopped as she waited to see what I would say. At that moment in my life I had to come to terms with the fact that as human beings we do not always know or understand the whys.

Finally, when I was able to speak, I shared with her how we had also prayed for Paul, loved him, and did not want to lose him. I told her that in this life we simply do not have all the answers. As Isaiah 55:8 says, *"For my thoughts are not your thoughts, neither are your ways my ways, saith the Lord."*

I told her of my Christian beliefs, and that while we did not always understand the workings of God, we could always be assured that He loves us and God's Word promises that He only allows what is best for us from an eternal perspective. We talked for what seemed like hours about our fears for our children suffering and possibly dying, along with the assurance we could have that if God chose to take them He had prepared a better place for them.

We could not sleep in the children's room because of fire regulations, so I would go into a small lounge nearby until I felt sure Paul was asleep for the night. As I sat on that old vinyl sofa in the lounge that night, I felt so overwhelmed by all the human suffering I had seen over the last few days. I felt helpless and frightened not only for our family but for all the families we had met.

I did not realize I was crying, but suddenly I heard myself instinctively cry out for my own mother, who had been dead for nine years. I felt like a little child again who needed to be comforted and assured that somehow everything would be all right. I sat there crying long into the night, praying for God to give me the strength to face all that was ahead and to help the other families around us.

On the day Paul was to be released from the hospital, the lady from the church came to pick us up. It had been a long day and Paul and I were both weary.

She took us to her home, gave us dinner and took us over to the apartment where we would stay. They had gone out that day and stocked the refrigerator for us. She showed me a phone they had installed in case we needed any emergency services or just wanted to call home. There was a lovely bedroom, bath, and living room with a beautiful fireplace, and filled with shelf after shelf of wonderful books.

This was just the home away from home I needed. After Paul drifted off to sleep at night, I would slip into the quiet of that beautiful living room, read a good book, and prepare myself spiritually and emotionally for the next day.

Rudy and Angie called regularly, and we tried to share with them the trials and triumphs of our days. On the days Paul felt good we would take in the local historic sites; he loved this just as much as I did. Other days we would go duck pin bowling or stop at a local restaurant for a hamburger or hot dog. It was important that he enjoy our stay as much as possible so he would not think only of the bad times.

On many days, as we sat waiting for Paul's turn to have his radiation, we would chat with other people in the waiting room. Paul became buddies with an older gentleman who was also having radiation therapy. I saw a strong bond develop between this executive of a large Boston firm and an eight-year-old boy because each understood what the other was going through.

The man's wife shared with me that he was suffering greatly from depression as part of his illness, and she was amazed at how his attitude changed after meeting Paul, who would tell him how Jesus loved him and that he was praying for him. It was strange to watch this relationship grow and see an eight-year-old provide strength and comfort for a 60-year-old man.

Siblings in a situation like ours are in a very difficult position. Though only ten years old, Angie tried to hide how hard all of this was for her. The family she stayed with took wonderful care of her, but she desperately missed being at home with her family.

At bedtime, when the lights went out, the loneliness would come down on her all at once. She cried almost every night, and the mother would rub her back for comfort until the tears stopped. This fine lady also shared with Angie how hard it was for her when her own father died while she was away at college.

Angie usually drifted off to sleep quoting Philippians 4:13. "*I can do all things through Christ who strengthens me.*" She did not want Rudy or me to know how hard this was for her because she did not want us to worry about her as she now realized how sick Paul really was. She asked her host family not to tell us about her tears. They had two small girls and their mother allowed Angie to share in their care. She grew to love those girls deeply, which gave her a sense of belonging. We thanked God for this precious family who provided Angie with love and security while we were in Boston.

Angie desperately wanted to come and visit us in Boston. She called one night crying, saying she was sick with the flu and wanted to come for a visit. I told her I was sorry but she could not come if she had the flu. Later that night her dad called back to say she did not actually have the flu but was really having a hard time being away from Paul and me. We felt it was important for her to come and visit, so she and Rudy flew up on a Wednesday afternoon and stayed until Sunday.

We had an interesting experience during her visit. Being from the South in a New England state, our accents were clearly different, and we got teased quite a bit. We had an equally difficult time understanding the locals as they dropped their "R"s.

A nurse at the hospital was chatting with Angie when suddenly the child got a funny look on her face. She hurried over to where we sat and said, "Mom, that nurse wanted to know if I went to the potty last night." Why would she ask a ten-year-old a question like that?

I chuckled as I explained to her that the previous night had been Halloween, and the nurse wanted to know if Angie had gone to the hospital party.

Seeing Paul undergo his radiation therapy and how sick it made him helped Angie understand more clearly that this was no vacation for him. She began to grasp what he was going through, and we saw sibling rivalry begin to disappear.

We knew one possible effect of the radiation was that Paul's tumor could swell due to irritation. At the onset of our fifth week Paul started to drag his right foot and slur his words. A CAT scan revealed that his tumor had swollen to the point that the doctors needed to add a wing to his shunt so it could carry the fluid off the brain. Paul had to go back into surgery and the treatments were stopped for a few days.

Rudy was scheduled to return to Boston during Thanksgiving week and meet with all of the doctors. Paul's neurologist and radiologist felt the radiation therapy had gone well, but we would need to come back the following April for additional CAT scans. Those films would show how successful the treatments had been.

With mixed feelings, I boarded the plane with Paul the Friday after Thanksgiving to return home. This trip had been extremely hard; many times during therapy Paul had been very sick. But we knew it was his only hope.

It had also been extremely difficult to share the sorrow of so many other families with ill children. Yet throughout our entire stay, God's miraculous peace had always been there for us. We had also seen Him provide our every need above and beyond what we deserved.

As we disembarked at the Roanoke airport, we saw a huge crowd of people and wondered what celebrity was on the plane. When Rudy, Paul and I came through the door everyone started clapping and waving signs that read, "Welcome Home." A red carpet rolled out to the front door where a limo waited to take us home. Our hearts were touched to see so many precious members of our church who had devoted their evening to this special welcome.

Paul rested and recuperated all of December but was anxious to return to school after Christmas break. When he did, he was able to keep up with his assignments but had little energy for anything else.

Paul loved to watch our Christian high school teams play basketball. One evening when he felt up to it, we thought we would take in a game. A highlight for him had always been at halftime after the floor was swept down, and the little guys in the stands would come down and try to shoot baskets until the teams came back out on the floor.

We were really surprised when on this night he said he wanted to shoot hoops with the other boys. He played around for three or four minutes before leaving the floor and coming back toward us. I could tell he was about to cry but would not let himself do so.

"Mom, why do I always have to be sick?" he whispered to me when he sat down.

I comforted him the best I could, but it was hard to say over and over again, "Honey, I don't know why."

Once more the earth began to turn green as spring arrived in full force — the time of year that always puts hope into our souls as the dreariness of winter gives way to new life.

As April approached, we were anxious to return to Boston and learn what the tests would reveal. Paul had gradually regained his strength, and we felt the tumor had reduced in size as the vomiting had stopped. That month we learned that it had shrunk from the size of a man's fist to that of a golf ball. He had two cysts as well, but the doctors felt the radiation would dry them up without any additional problems.

We joyfully left Boston, feeling that possibly we had won the war with this brain tumor and started to pull our lives together again.

During the summer the hardest thing for Paul to deal with was that most of the time he did not feel like playing with his friends. He had always looked forward to playing basketball as he got older, but now the loss of his peripheral vision prevented him from seeing the ball as it was thrown to him. This was hard for him and Rudy, as both had looked forward to Rudy teaching him to play.

CHAPTER 6
Deep Valley

As July approached, Angie, Paul and I anxiously awaited our vacation with Rudy's parents and his sister's family at Nags Head, North Carolina. My love for walks on the beach, riding the waves, and the warmth of the sun had been passed on to my children.

Rudy did not share our enthusiasm. For him the beach meant sunburn and sand in your shoes. As with most families at vacation time, we had to find areas of compromise. So for a whole week Rudy had the joy of not shaving, just generally looking sloppy, and fishing from the pier or in the surf. Fishing is not my thing; I cannot stand to touch any form of live bait or take a hook out of a poor fish's mouth. So I would sit on the pier with Rudy and watch the waves or the masses of people, or play with the children in the surf. This allowed us to enjoy our vacation as a family.

A week before we were to leave, I was driving around trying to finish buying all the odds and ends needed in sportswear and swimsuits so we would be ready to go. Angie and Paul rode in the back seat. When I looked in the rear view mirror to talk to them, I noticed Paul looking strange, as if his body were drifting off to the left. I thought he was sleepy and asked if he wanted to go home.

"No, I am not sleepy at all," he said.

Then why was he sitting like that? My heart skipped a beat.

"Paul, sit up straight," I said.

He shifted himself, and I watched carefully through the mirror as his body started to drift to the left again. I was very concerned about what was going on but did not want to upset the children, so I told them it was getting late and we had better call it a day.

When Rudy got home from work, he sensed something was wrong. We told the children to go outside and play while I fixed dinner. As soon as the door closed behind them, I told Rudy what had happened in the car with Paul.

We sat down at the table, both of us wondering if this could possibly be related to Paul's tumor. He had not become symptomatic with head-aches or lethargy, but he did have bouts of hiccups that lasted for hours. A terrible uneasiness crept over us but we tried not to panic before we could talk with Paul's doctor. We did not sleep well that night; it seemed as though morning would never come.

As soon as the neurosurgeon's office opened, I called his nurse and told her about Paul's symptoms and asked if we could get an appoint-ment. When we pulled into his parking lot later that day, all I could think about was sitting in our car a year earlier and trying to cope with the doctor's warning that Paul would die from his tumor.

"Lord, we thought we were going to lose Paul, but found hope through the radiation program at Boston Children's Hospital," I prayed. "We got a good report in April. Please don't let something else happen to him."

As we waited, I looked around at the patients and their families and felt deep compassion for them, as I had learned how much an entire family suffers when one member is desperately ill.

Finally they called us in, and the doctor conducted a neurological exam. He told Rudy and me that the tests didn't indicate any serious problems, although he was concerned about Paul's balance and the prolonged bouts of hiccups. But he did not feel it was serious enough for a CAT scan at that time.

We told the doctor we would cancel our vacation plans for the next week, but he emphasized that, whatever Paul's condition, we should let him live the most full and productive life he could. He felt the vacation would be good for all of us.

I remember every single detail of our vacation that year.

Rudy never liked to miss a Sunday morning at our church, so whenever possible he preached before we left for vacation. After the morning service Angie and Paul were jumping up and down in their eagerness to head for the beach, as Rudy's family was already there.

Monday, Tuesday, and Wednesday were glorious days. We rode waves, made sand castles, walked the beach and swam with the kids in the pool. Paul and Angie loved to swim, and they and their cousins would play every imaginable water game for hours on end. They would not give up the day until they fell asleep from exhaustion after a long, busy day.

Paul did not jump out of bed Thursday morning when the other kids did. I went in to check on him and he said he didn't feel well.

"Just get some rest," I told him. "You've been playing hard these past three days."

He did not want to miss any of the fun with the other children, but I could tell that he just didn't feel like getting up. We readied the other children and they soon left for the beach with Rudy's mother and sister.

Around midmorning Paul finally got up. "I don't feel like going to the ocean," he said. "But I'd like to go out to the pool."

Just as we got outside Angie and her cousins returned from the beach to swim in the pool as well. When Paul got in we noticed he had difficulty keeping his balance. We did not want to upset him so both Rudy and I got in the pool so we could watch him closely. We played games with him until he tired. In spite of his illness, he pushed himself to do everything like the other children.

After lunch Paul wanted to take a nap. As he lay there that afternoon sleeping, I sat on the bed with him and rubbed his back while tears flowed down my face. I prayed that nothing else was happening with the tumor, for we had done everything humanly possible to fight it.

He awoke completely refreshed and was raring to go to the amusement park after dinner. The children ran from one ride to the other squealing with delight as the rides went faster and faster. They were having a delightful time, and all of them said they wanted to ride the Tilt-a-Whirl. Paul did not want to ride with two yucky girls, so I said I would ride with him.

We laughed with glee as we spun around when he suddenly grabbed his head. It scared me nearly to death, but he said it was all right as the ride came to a close. As we got off the ride I noticed he had wet his pants and apparently did not even realize it. I told Rudy and the rest of the family that Paul and I were going back to the motel for the evening. Paul wanted to stay and ride with his sister and cousins but he just did not feel up to it. I gave him a bath and put him down for the night.

Neither Rudy nor I could sleep that night. We hated to cut short Paul's vacation but with these new developments we felt we must take him back to see the doctor.

Paul seemed restless during the night, and when he awoke the next morning he was upset that he had wet the bed while he slept. He didn't feel good, but he certainly didn't want to leave the beach and go see the doctor. I prepared his breakfast, and he seemed to have difficulty chewing. This concerned us enough that we decided to stop at the University of Virginia Hospital, which was much closer.

When we loaded the car and started to leave, everyone tried hard not to cry. All of the adults were so concerned and wondering what was happening to Paul. The children did not fully understand so they cried because we had to leave early. It was also hard for us to drive away and leave Angie again.

Paul slept most of the way to the hospital and when he awoke he said he felt fine and did not want to go in and see the doctors. We promised him that if he would be patient long enough to let them examine him we would take him out for hot dogs. Little did we know as we walked into that hospital building that we would never get to keep our promise to him.

We asked to see Paul's pediatric endocrinologist, who was familiar with his case, and explained to her everything that had happened to him the preceding 24 hours. She ran some blood work and there were no problems with his electrolytes, but she did pick up on some additional deficits when she and her staff did the neurological exam.

The endocrinologist was not at all sure what was going on with Paul. She felt we needed to call in the heads of the neurosurgery and neurology departments to evaluate him. It was late in the afternoon when they finished with all the tests. The CAT scan revealed that the tumor appeared to be the same size but the cysts were no longer visible.

The neurosurgeon explained that they felt there were three possible explanations for the deterioration Paul was experiencing: the tumor had fingers growing down into the brain; the cysts had ruptured and caused chemical meningitis; or the large doses of radiation he had received were destroying good cells in the brain. No matter which of the three were actually happening, they said there was nothing else they could do for Paul. We would just have to wait and see.

When they finally brought Paul back to the room he was exhausted from all of the tests and fell into a fitful sleep. Rudy and I stayed with him all through the night trying to make him as comfortable as possible. As soon as the early morning came, we began to call family members and Christian people all over the country asking them to pray for Paul.

Soon the neurologists and neurosurgeons came to check on him. He was beginning to walk on his tiptoes as his heel cords were tightening from the brain damage. Over the next few days he lost a lot of ground very quickly.

His little body became more and more rigid and his temperature would go from subnormal to a very elevated level. He began to have terrible muscle spasms. His arms and legs would draw so tight that he would scream for hours in pain until they could finally give him enough medication to relax his body. He became less and less responsive.

The doctors began to have serious problems controlling Paul's electrolytes, as his sodium would drop to dangerously low levels. Soon he was on IVs around the clock which enabled the doctors to maintain a closer control on his intake and output.

Precious people wrote, called and came to visit each day and share how churches and individuals all over the nation were praying for us. Our hearts were deeply touched by the love shown for Paul and our family during this time. Without their encouragement and support I do not think I could have survived the horrible fear that gripped my heart each time Paul's temperature soared or he screamed from pain with muscle spasms.

Eventually Paul slipped into a coma and could not respond to us in any way. We would read to him, play his favorite tapes or just whisper in his ear of our love and how much we wanted him to come back to us.

When Angie came to visit Paul this time it was extremely hard for her. When she waved goodbye to her brother at the beach he was a totally normal little boy. Now her brother did not open his eyes or speak, even when she stood there and pleaded with him to say something. When the body spasms would start, she would stand by him and rub his legs as long as the spasms lasted. We did everything possible to help her understand what was happening and explained that the doctors were doing all they could.

The doctors were still conducting tests daily, trying to decide what had happened to Paul. Almost hourly a group of doctors and residents came in to examine him and discuss their findings. Rudy and I became more and more upset at what we felt was a lack of sensitivity for our feelings as a family, not to mention a total disregard for the possibility that Paul might be able to understand part of what they were saying.

Finally, another group paraded through with their idea of some treatment they felt should be tried on Paul, as if Rudy and I were not even sitting there. Suddenly Rudy stood up and ordered them out of the room. He told them that no residents would decide on any treatment for our son. We had no objection to the fact that residents had to be trained, but we were not accustomed to their making decisions except under the direction of the doctor in charge.

They looked quite startled that anyone would question them, but Rudy responded, "You are totally out of line!"

He immediately went to the head of pediatrics and told him we would allow residents to learn from Paul, but they could only ask questions. All future treatments would be discussed with us only through our primary doctor.

Previously we always had wonderfully considerate doctors who showed respect and concern for us, and it had taken a lot of inappropriate behavior on the part of these doctors for us to speak out. Most people felt like we did that doctors are above reproach, but we soon learned to ask direct questions so we could always be fully aware of any treatments Paul was going to have.

To use this unpleasant experience for a positive change, Rudy met with the head of pediatrics to share how families feel when doctors do not properly interact with them in a teaching hospital. The hospital was still using the information to help train residents the last time we visited there.

The end of the summer brought with it Paul's birthday — August 18, 1981. Somehow I just knew he would come out of the coma for his birthday. All day long we talked about his birthday, read his cards to him and sang "Happy Birthday" to him. As the day drew to a close, Rudy and I became quieter and the tears soon began to roll down my face. Rudy came over and held me.

"I just knew that some way Paul would come back to us today," I sobbed.

As Paul's coma dragged on a terrible feeling of despair overtook us. We were exhausted, but when we dozed off for a few minutes we had horrible nightmares. I especially would awaken with panic attacks, feeling as if my heart would burst out of my chest.

Angie had been able to stay in town with us since school was not in session. We had let her come to see Paul daily, but she was so upset to see her little brother unable to respond in any way. Soon we felt it better if she did not come so often.

The next week Rudy had to leave us to take care of his responsibilities at the church, and we thought it was best for Angie to go stay with Rudy's parents. We had no idea how long Paul would stay in a coma.

Suddenly one Sunday morning Paul's body began to have violent tremors, and I called for the nurses. By the time the nurses got there Paul was having a grand mal seizure. I had never seen a seizure before and it was one of the most frightening things I have ever endured. It only lasted a few minutes but it seemed like an eternity to me.

Finally they got it stopped. I stood there trembling, praying that Paul would never have another seizure when Rudy's parents walked in. I was so happy to have them with me because only a few minutes later Paul went into another violent seizure. This time it would not stop, and we were asked to step outside the room.

Paul's doctor came out to tell us they could not get the seizure under control and his vital signs were not good, so we needed to be prepared for the worst. I asked the nurse to keep calling Rudy until he got home from church to tell him to come as soon as possible.

As we waited in the hall, I prayed and asked the Lord to take care of Paul. I just knew we were going to lose him, but I begged God to spare him until Rudy could get there. I feared that if Paul died while Rudy was preaching he would always suffer guilt even though he could not possibly stay at the hospital all the time.

Paul's doctor came out to give us a report, and I asked him to let me go back in the room. He said I could, but it would be very distressing to see all of the tubes and monitors. None of that mattered as long as I could be close to my son. Each time as the digital readout on Paul's heart monitor showed his heart rate getting faster and faster, I thought he surely could not live through this much longer.

The afternoon wore on, and more doctors came in trying to get the horrible seizures to stop, but nothing worked.

Rudy's father was waiting for him when he got off the elevator. He told Rudy how bad things were and that he had better get himself together so he could be strong for me. Rudy went to the chapel and asked God to give him strength for all that was ahead. When Rudy came to Paul's room, I thanked the Lord for allowing him to get there before something happened to Paul.

Late into the night the seizures finally stopped, and his vital signs began to stabilize. We had made it through one more crisis. Paul was now in a very deep coma and totally unresponsive to any stimulus.

My sister, Barbara, had come to stay at the hospital with me. My family is very close and she talked lovingly to Paul, urging him to get better so he could come visit his cousins in Tennessee.

The Lord provided comfort and strength to us through family, friends, Christian doctors and nurses on the hospital staff, and our personal prayer and devotional time. Many times when everything was quiet in Paul's room a verse from a beautiful hymn would go through my mind and provide comfort.

Paul began to come around a little at the end of August. He was not totally out of the coma, but the hospital staff felt we could take him home with around-the-clock nursing care.

I worried about the tremendous amount of responsibility this was putting on Rudy. He was trying to carry out his duties at the church, go to Lynchburg to pick up Angie so they could come to the hospital and visit us, and work with the insurance company to find out the services for which they would be responsible. Now he had to get all of the equipment to set up a "hospital" room in our home.

He spent days purchasing necessary medical supplies as well as renting a hospital bed, wheelchair and suction machine. Securing nursing care took a lot of time as he had to coordinate three eight-hour shifts seven days a week. Finally, all of the preparations were made and we secured a registered nurse and an emergency vehicle to come and transport us home.

As I prepared to leave the hospital with Paul, I was so thankful to be able to go home with my family. Rudy's parents had done a wonderful job watching Angie but it was time for school to start and she wanted to be at her own house. We were so concerned how all of this confusion was affecting her and wanted to get her settled back into her home.

Yet, as the discharge day approached, I found myself feeling insecure about leaving the hospital. The doctors were still not certain what had happened to Paul. Most of them leaned toward chemical meningitis resulting from the ruptured cysts. Could we adequately take care of Paul away from the hospital environment? We all knew how difficult his profound electrolyte imbalance was to manage. I knew we would need great strength from the Lord to face this new challenge.

As we rode away from the hospital that afternoon, I remembered how Paul had walked into that same hospital just one month before — a lively, happy eight-year-old whose only desire was to hurry and see the doctors so he could get a hot dog. We were unable to keep that promise and I wondered if Paul would ever again eat a hot dog, swim in a pool, or ride at an amusement park.

My heart felt so heavy, and at times I felt angry at what seemed like such an unfair turn of events in Paul's illness. Rudy and I wanted to show our love for the Savior in the bad times as well as the good, so I tried to make myself think of all the wonderful times we had enjoyed together.

I prayed as we drove away, "God, no matter what comes, help us not to become bitter, but only better for you."

CHAPTER 7
Adjusting at Home

As the ambulance pulled up to our home, I wavered between joy and sadness. I was so thankful to have Paul home, but my mind went back to a month earlier when Angie and Paul were jumping with excitement as we loaded the car for our vacation. Now we were bringing Paul home in a coma-like state, and that first day of vacation seemed so long ago.

Our church had prepared lunch for us, and friends stopped by to welcome us home. The registered nurse was there to help with Paul. After we gave him a small amount of fluids and changed his diapers, we got him settled for a nap.

We sat down with our friends and tried to eat lunch, but we were so overwhelmed by the drastic change in Paul that none of us really ate much. Our considerate friends tried to help us by joking around, but they were also so shaken that it was tough to get through the meal.

After they left, Paul settled down a little and went to sleep, so Rudy suggested we all try to rest for a little while. I lay down, but my fear of failing to adequately care for Paul outside the hospital increased by the minute. We did not have accurate enough scales to measure the urine in his diapers, and how would we ever get him to take in enough fluids without the IVs? On many occasions during the last month I had seen Paul almost die, and something kept nagging at me that everything was not all right.

"Try to get some rest, dear," Rudy said as I started to get up to check on Paul.

"Honey, I can't sleep," I said. "I am too worried about Paul."

When I got downstairs his nurse said he was OK, so we just sat beside his bed. In just a few minutes his eyes pulled to one side and he started a violent seizure. We breathlessly waited for it to stop, but it got stronger and stronger. He began to lose his color, so we quickly called the rescue squad.

It seemed like an eternity before they got there. On the way to the hospital the paramedics gave Paul oxygen to be sure he was getting enough.

At the emergency room the seizures would not stop, and blood tests showed Paul's sodium level to be extremely high. They put IVs in to try and get his electrolytes to a normal level, but his body was going through violent convulsions. The doctor told us Paul might not make it through the night.

He planned to transfer him to the Neurological Intensive Care Unit so he could be monitored as closely as possible. I asked the doctor not to put Paul anywhere that we could not stay with him. When we promised to honor their request that we stay beside his bed out of the way of the nurses and leave immediately when asked due to emergencies, they allowed us to accompany him to the NICU.

We sat by Paul's bed and prayed, asking God to stop the seizure so his little body could get some rest. We prayed for God to have His will concerning Paul but, of course, we desperately wanted him to live. It was in the wee hours of the morning when they were finally able to get the seizure to stop.

When one of us stepped out to the waiting room to give friends and family a report on Paul, it amazed us to see how many people had stopped by to check on him and leave word of prayers and encouragement for our family.

The physicians could not believe Paul had lived through the night. They started tests to see if they could get any response from him, but Paul did not respond in any way to pain, light or sound. The staff informed us that he was suffering from severe brain deterioration.

When we went to the cafeteria and tried to eat, it seemed so strange to me that the world was just going on at a normal everyday pace when our little boy was upstairs dying. Day became night and then day again without any significant change, and since the hospital needed Paul's NICU bed we were moved back to a regular room with nursing care around the clock.

Rudy and I had to start dividing our time between home and the hospital. As Rudy's mother had to return to her home, one of us had to be home with Angie after school and Rudy had to work. One dreary, rainy morning I relieved Rudy at about 6:00 a.m. at the hospital so he could go home, shower and be on our church's radio program at 7:45 a.m. He had been working, helping with Angie, and coming to the hospital every free minute.

We heard the physicians tell us time and time again that Paul was terminal, but as parents we would never give up hope until his last breath. His little body was so rigid and drawing up tighter each day. He had total foot drop because his heel cords were so drawn. Physical therapists were using splints on his hands to prevent them from contracting back under his wrists.

We played music for Paul, read him stories, told him about everything that was happening and asked him to blink his eyes for us.

After about two weeks we had absolutely no response from Paul in any way. I rubbed his legs and feet hoping to relieve some of the pain from the muscle spasms. Out of habit, when I rubbed his left foot I asked him to move his big toe. One time I thought I saw it move ever so slightly but was not certain.

I excitedly called for Rudy and the nurse to come and see. Again I held his foot and asked him to move his big toe, and to our amazement we saw the slightest movement. We hugged each other as well as Paul, crying and praising the Lord that Paul could hear and obey a command.

We requested permission from the doctor to start trying to rehabilitate Paul. The doctors felt very apprehensive about giving us any encouragement since they felt he was terminal, but they consented to have physical and speech therapy started and also gave permission for us to start trying to get him up into a chair.

Paul could not support his head so we would lift him onto a chair, put a band around his forehead and tie it around the back of the chair. The physical therapy was all passive, but at least they were able to stop his body from contracting any tighter.

In an attempt to teach him to take some nourishment, his speech therapist had us take a small sucker, dip it into water and rub it on Paul's tongue. At first any moisture would choke him, but we worked day after day until he finally could swallow a drop or two without coughing. We were then able to move up to slivers of ice.

Paul had a naso-gastric tube for feeding, but the nurse started feeding him half-strength milk shakes through a premature baby bottle nipple. His tongue and throat muscles were so weak that it was an extremely slow process.

He was still having horrible muscle spasms and would scream with pain until they stopped. He required so much care that the nurses, Rudy and I worked with him constantly, around the clock — trying to get him to take enough liquid to have his feeding tube removed; meticulously measuring all intake and output; exercising him and trying to rub his little arms and legs when the spasms hit.

Angie came to the hospital as often as possible. She would sit on the bed with Paul and tell him about all the kids at school, read to him, and help massage his legs when the spasms hit. This was so hard for her, but she desperately wanted to help her little brother come home.

Paul had been in the hospital for about three weeks when our endocrinologist and neurologist said we could possibly take him home in a week or two if his electrolytes remained stable, and if we could get his intake up to between 800 and 1,000 cc in a 24-hour period. We worked and prayed so hard for Paul to be able to come home. Even if we had to have nurses at home around the clock, we felt we needed to be at home with Angie.

About ten days later the doctors released Paul. As we parked in our driveway, I wondered how long we would get to stay this time. We tried to settle into some kind of schedule for our family with nurses and therapists constantly coming and going.

Paul was still having horrible muscle spasms and would scream with the pain day and night. Due to the brain damage, he had no definite sleep patterns and would usually sleep for an hour or so at the most before the spasms would hit again. He also seemed to have some discomfort in his head and would pull at his ears and whine with pain again.

Many nights I would lie awake waiting for Rudy to fall asleep so I could slip back downstairs and help with Paul. Even though intellectually I knew I did not have the medical training or the ability to stay awake 24 hours a day to care for him, I found it difficult to let someone else do it. He was my child, and I wanted to take care of him.

The Lord gave us precious Christian nurses who were themselves mothers. They could sense how difficult this was for me. Many times after I came downstairs to sit with them they would urge me to try to get some rest, promising to call me immediately at even a small change. I would drag myself upstairs, but I hated to go to sleep because I knew the nightmares and anxiety attacks would start. I would awaken from a deep sleep with my heart pounding, feeling that something was terribly wrong.

As my mind cleared, the reality of Paul's condition overpowered me. Fears and doubts that could be handled during the day grew into frightening monsters at night. Most nights I would try to calm myself by quoting Scriptures and talking with the Lord, but many times I would have to wake Rudy. Some nights he would just hold me close and I would fall back asleep, but many nights he had to let me talk through my fears.

Each family member deals with trauma in his or her own way. We talked with Angie about our hopes for Paul to improve and we tried not to let her know how much we were hurting. She also held in a lot of her fears and anxieties, not wanting to add to our burden. Also, in her mind no difficulty she experienced could possibly measure up to what Paul was going through, so she felt she shouldn't talk about it.

Rudy had many wonderful pastor friends with whom he could talk about Paul, and he is by nature more open with his feelings than I am. I did not share my feelings with anyone except Rudy because I felt people were looking to me as the pastor's wife to be strong. I had no idea how desperately our church members and friends wanted to help but didn't have the opportunity because I always acted like I was in control. Little did they know that I would leave home crying every Sunday morning and stop just one block from the church to give myself a stern lecture, freshen my makeup and put on a brave smile. By not acknowledging my pain and reaching out to others, I robbed my friends of the privilege of ministering to me. Nor did they fell free to admit their own struggles and to receive help from me.

We had been home for about eight weeks when Rudy said he was going to take me out for a meal. At this point I had barely left Paul except to go to church. I assured him I'd rather stay at home, but he was emphatic that he wanted me to go. We discussed this to the point that I became angry at him for insisting that I go.

When I finally gave in, by the time we left I had told the nurses at least five times where we were going and what the telephone number was. When we got to the restaurant I had worked myself into such a frenzy, and I began to cry. I was able to eat only a few bites, but Rudy encouraged me to stay at least for a while.

The moment we got home I started to jump out of the car, but Rudy said he needed to talk with me. In the privacy of our car we both reminisced about how much we missed Paul running through the house, playing ball with his dad, trying to talk us out of making him try different vegetables, his beautiful blond hair, the sparkle in his big brown eyes, sitting in Rudy's office chair assuring us that one day he would be a preacher like Daddy, playing gleefully with Angie, swimming in the pool, fussing with Angie, his sweet and earnest prayers, singing "Jesus Loves Me," riding his green machine, aggravating his sister, playing chess with anyone who would challenge him to a game, going out on the bus route to talk to boys and girls about Jesus, jumping on his bed until I stepped into the room, going to McDonald's for a burger and fries, dressing up like Batman, playing cops and robbers with his buddies, asking for candy at the grocery store every week, eating hot dogs, complaining about having to take a bath, fussing if he got his hair cut at a beauty salon and not a barber shop, riding the waves at the beach, playing after church with his friends, and a hundred other things.

Would we ever again have that Paul, or had God given us a very different Paul to love and care for?

We were also very concerned about how to help Angie cope with all of these changes. She needed to be able to have some sort of normal 11-year-old girl's life. We wanted to be sure she knew her needs were very important to us and to encourage her to tell us openly how she felt about Paul's illness.

Rudy and I have been best friends since we met in college, and we so missed having time to sit and talk privately. With people constantly in our home and the other demands on our time there seemed to be no time left to sit and talk without interruption. We both missed this special time so much.

The counselors at the hospital said statistics show couples who deal with long-term catastrophic illness in the family have a divorce rate of about 80 percent. We wanted so much to draw closer during this time instead of letting all of the stress drive a wedge between us. We pledged to be constantly aware of this danger.

I told Rudy I was sorry for being so resistant to go out with him that night because I could see how carefully we would have to be to guard this beautiful relationship we had shared for 14 years.

Rudy then brought up a very touchy subject. He said I had to begin to accept the help the Lord had given us through the nurses. He understood how hard it was for me to let someone else care for Paul, but at some point I had to get some consistent rest.

I knew it had been months since I had slept through the entire night, and such an erratic schedule was taking its toll on my body. Every time I ate I had terrible pain in my stomach. The doctor had to give me medicine for colitis, but he informed me the problem would not go away until I got out from under some of the stress. I knew how important it was for me to watch my health so I could take care of my responsibilities. The Lord would have to help me surrender in this area because it was so difficult for me.

It was getting late and we had to go into the house. We knew the road ahead of us was filled with much uncertainty. How much could Paul come back mentally and physically? Would he ever walk or talk? Would he ever be able to go back to school? How could we handle all of this financially? How would it affect our church?

All that seemed to loom on the horizon were questions. This was much too heavy a burden for us, and our only comfort was that we knew our Savior would walk each step with us.

That night as I drifted off to sleep, I reread some of the beautiful cards we had received and found just the comfort I needed from the one entitled "Footprints," containing the words of a poem written by Mary Stevenson in the 1930s. It read:

> "One night I dreamed I was walking along the beach with the Lord. Many scenes from my life flashed across the sky. Sometimes there were two sets of footprints; at other times only one. This bothered me because I noticed that during the low periods of my life — when I was suffering from anguish, sorrow or defeat — I could see only one set of footprints.
>
> "So I said to the Lord, 'You promised me that if I followed You, You would walk with me always. But I have noticed that during the most trying periods in my life there has been

only one set of footprints in the sand. Why, when I have needed You most, have You not been there with me?'

"The Lord replied, 'During your times of trial and suffering, when you see only one set of footprints — it was then that I carried you.'"

CHAPTER 8
Bitter Pill

The brilliant red and yellow leaves on the tree outside Paul's window indicated summer had slipped into fall.

Paul's doctors were still highly uncertain about his prognosis. The CAT scan did show that a large portion of the left hemisphere of his brain had been destroyed when the cysts ruptured. We took heart from medical reports that sometimes a healthy part of the brain would take over some functions of a damaged part. We held onto this hope tenaciously.

The doctors stressed to us often the severity of the damage to Paul's brain but encouraged us to try an active rehabilitation program with him. "You can never predict the outcome of these cases," they told us.

Some days we had an ecstatic hope that with enough love, care and work, we could bring Paul back to a normal state. On other days, when we observed his extremely limited abilities, we feared he would never be any better.

Paul was still in diapers with no bowel or bladder control. We began the task of retraining him by sitting him on a bedside commode chair, much like a two-year-old, then returning him to bed. When the nurse felt it was time for him to go again, we transferred him and let him sit there as long as he was able. When he was successful, we rewarded him with a lot of praise. We knew bladder (and especially bowel) control was a long shot, but we rejoiced each time he used the bedside chair.

Another result of the brain injury was that Paul had almost total foot-drop. His heel cords drew up, making him walk on his tiptoes. The heel cords would have to be lengthened before he could ever walk again, but he was too weak to endure such surgery.

The other option was to use serial plaster-casting to stretch his heel cords. The doctors and nurses pushed on his little feet as hard as they could stretch them and put the casts on. This procedure hurt Paul, but we knew the heel cords had to be stretched if he had any hope of walking again. Each week they cut off the cast, pushed his feet up a few degrees farther and put on a new cast.

This courageous little boy's progress came very slowly, but each day brought some small improvements. Paul's home care nurse, Iris, had worked with neurological patients for years. "Don't expect improvements by leaps and bounds, but celebrate each baby step of accomplishment," she told us.

It was difficult to evaluate what Paul could understand because he did not talk, and we were not certain how good his vision was. His speech therapist worked to strengthen his throat and tongue muscles to help him talk.

October 16, 1981, was a red-letter day for us. With a beautiful smile on her face, Iris called me into Paul's room and said, "Paul has something to say."

Slowly but surely, across his lips came the most beautiful word I had ever heard: "MAMA!"

If a heart could burst with joy, I surely thought mine would. Paul wore a little smile as though he sensed our pride in him. With a lot of prodding Paul was able to say it again for his dad to hear when he came home for lunch.

Since the brain cyst rupture, Paul's eye muscles had gotten so weak that his eyes would drift to the right and stay fixed in that position. By this time his eye muscles were strong enough to keep his eyes focused, but we still could not tell how much he could see.

Iris began bringing Paul to the table for meals. One morning she dropped a small white pill on our kitchen table. Before she could find it Paul slowly extended his hand and picked it up for her. We praised the Lord for that evidence that Paul's vision was better than we had ever hoped.

Our house resembled a kindergarten classroom. Everyone wore name tags and everything in the house had a label on it. For instance, guests often wondered why we would need a big sign labeled "Refrigerator" taped on our refrigerator. We explained that Paul needed as many reinforcements as possible to help with his vocabulary.

The Lord in His perfect will had provided just what we needed with regard to Paul's nurses. Iris was extremely knowledgeable in rehabilitative nursing, but she also taught us the real meaning of words such as "patience" and "understanding." She would work for an hour trying to get Paul to put on one sock. His little fingers could barely scratch at it, but with her extreme patience he finally got the sock pulled part of the way up.

Paul's second-shift nurse, Mary Ann, had been very reluctant to nurse a child as ill as Paul in a home setting. When I called to ask her to work for us she insisted, "I do not prefer to do home care."

I did not know if I was talking with a Christian or not, but I poured my heart out to her. "The hospital staff recommended you and said that you would be wonderful to work with Paul. We are praying you will take the case," I said.

She said she didn't think she would do it, but she would consider it and call me back the next day. When she called back, she said, "I don't know why I am doing this, but I will nurse Paul until you can find someone else."

Once she started, she became such a part of the team in our rehab efforts that she had no desire to leave. Mary Ann bubbled over with sunshine and the joy of living. Her infectious laughter and love of life soon won her a young friend in Angie. Many times as I slipped into Paul's room I heard Mary Ann answer Angie's childlike questions and reassure her that everyone was doing everything possible to help Paul.

In her wisdom, Mary Ann sensed how much Angie wanted to partici-pate in Paul's program. She let her massage Paul's legs during the spasms, read to him, and work with his math and reading cue cards. This drew Angie and Paul closer together. It was still so hard for any of us to accept the drastic changes in Paul, and the only way we could cope was by pour-ing ourselves into helping him as much as possible.

God's love was evident to us through Paul's nurses as well as our many friends. People constantly stopped by to visit. I could tell that it was extremely difficult for them to see Paul in diapers, with casts on his legs, and unable to verbally respond to their conversations. It was just too painful for some visitors, and I knew they would not be able to come back. Later they shared with mutual friends that they couldn't deal with seeing Paul because it made them realize the possibility of something happening to one of their own children. Other friends seemed deter-mined to dig in their heels and help; they came again and again despite the emotional pain.

Paul progressed to the point that he needed to go to the hospital and use their equipment for physical therapy. After a couple of days the thera-pist said we would have to bring him in before the hospital's inpatients came down. Because his little body was so rigid, he screamed with pain during the therapy and this upset the other patients to the point that they could not go through with their own therapy.

Iris and I exercised Paul at home during the day. One day he screamed with such pain I couldn't stand it. I ran upstairs so shaken that I just dropped to my knees and angrily cried out, "How much more can he endure? Why, God, why? It isn't fair for an innocent child to suffer like this!"

The day before I had gone shopping and was waiting for the store clerk to help me. I saw a mother with a little boy who looked so much like Paul and thought, "How fortunate this lady is to have such a beauti-ful and healthy child."

From their conversation I understood that this boy and his mother had been out for quite a while, and she had promised earlier they would make no more stops as he was tired and hungry. He began to cry to go home, and she jerked him up and shook him, saying, "Shut up! I'll go when I'm good and ready!"

Suddenly I felt like I wanted to grab her and tell her that she had better not treat him like that ever again. I wanted to scream at her about how fortunate she was to have him. When she realized that someone was staring at her and saw the look on my face, she started apologizing to him.

I was so upset that I left the store without picking up what I had gone in there for. When Rudy noticed I was much quieter than usual that night, he asked what was wrong and I told him about the incident in the store.

"Why would God give such a precious child to a woman like that?" I asked.

We talked for hours that night about understanding why bad things happen to God's people. I know God's ways are above our ways and He can see from beginning to end, but these truths brought little comfort to me that night.

It was so frustrating for us trying to straighten out all of the hospital, doctor, lab and therapy bills. Bills arrived every day, and most of the time the insurance company only paid a portion of them. I spent hours resubmitting claims to the insurance company and trying to set up payment plans that our budget could handle.

The weeks of stress took its toll on our family. We each tried to act cheerful and positive in front of one another, yet we cringed in the face of reality as we saw the extent of Paul's brain damage.

As the dark days of winter set in, I lived in fear that our lives would never be the same again. I went through the normal functions of the day, but it seemed that a big cloud loomed over our home all the time. Rudy and I ached to have Paul run, jump, giggle, play and be able to do all of the things he could do before. It was so hard to go to Sunday school and church and leave him at home with the nurse. We had always enjoyed family togetherness, and we had to force ourselves to go to necessary activities and not be able to take him. What if he could never go with us or participate in our lives as before? We knew we had to accept this possibility, and it was a bitter pill to swallow.

The Thanksgiving holiday was coming quickly. How could we celebrate, especially with Paul like this? It was also difficult to cope with the constant despair that always seemed just beneath the surface. We could not seem to break its hold on us.

A favorite verse of mine has always been James 1:5. *"If any of you lack wisdom, let him ask of God, that giveth to all men liberally, and upbraideth not; and it shall be given him."* One morning I begged God for some of that wisdom to understand what was happening to our family.

Later that morning as I straightened up the den a TV talk show was discussing a subject relatively new to me at that time, Alzheimer's disease. I noticed that many of the family members and care givers wore the same look of despair that I saw in the mirror and on Angie and Rudy's faces. The interviewer asked each person what was the hardest thing they experienced in dealing with this disease.

One elderly gentleman responded, "I miss my wife."

Everyone seemed puzzled, but he explained that the disease had taken the wife he had known for more than 30 years and given him a distinctly different wife to care for and love. "You see, I am grieving the loss of my wife as I knew her," he said.

All of a sudden my answer was there. Our family was grieving the loss of the son and brother we had known for nine years. God had taken our normal Paul and given us a mentally and physically handicapped Paul to care for and love.

I was thankful that Iris and Paul were at therapy because the realization of this loss brought forth cries of anguish from the depths of my soul. I stayed upstairs in my room all day, letting the held-back tears from the past months flow freely. I alternated between sobbing and praying, asking God to help Rudy and me accept this and do all we needed to do to help Angie and Paul through all that we faced.

Rudy could tell I had been crying when he came home that night. As he sat down to talk to me, he related an incident that occurred that morning while he was driving Angie to school.

We had been praying for a bereaved family that morning at the breakfast table. As they drove to school, Angie told her dad that she understood how that family felt to have someone close die. Rudy asked her how she could understand this, since we had not lost any family members since she was old enough to remember.

"Oh yes, Daddy, I have," she said, "because Paul died."

Rudy was shocked. "Angie, Paul did not die."

"Yes, Daddy, he did," she answered emphatically. "God took my little brother that I have grown up with and gave me a new little brother to love and help, but he is not the same brother."

God revealed to her little heart just as He had to mine that we would never have our Paul back as we had known him.

As Rudy and I sat talking that night, we came to grips with the reality that our lives would never return to "normal." We were so afraid of all that lay ahead, but we felt we could somehow go through the days with the strength we received from the Lord, each other, our families, our church, and our many friends.

CHAPTER 9
The Holiday Season

We struggled daily to cope with the multitude of problems Paul now had.

Due to pituitary gland damage, his other endocrine glands did not produce the hormones his body needed for regulation. One in particular was the anti-diuretic hormone the kidneys require to reabsorb the water needed for the body. As a result, Paul produced large volumes of urine and suffered intense thirst. It broke our hearts to hear him beg for water day and night.

Each of Paul's doctors and nurses were kind, compassionate, caring men and women who worked tirelessly to help care for Paul. His endocrinologist kept in constant contact with the nurses. Through blood tests and their careful records of intake and output, he finally developed a dosage that eased Paul's insatiable thirst to some degree. We praised God for these men and women who, after years of training and study, gave of themselves willingly to help us care for our son.

Having someone in our home 24 hours a day was still a struggle for us. We missed the freedom to sit at the dinner table or in the den and freely discuss family matters. It continued to be hard for me to accept others caring for Paul; although the nurses did everything they could to help us integrate Paul into our daily lives as much possible.

As the weeks progressed, I became more acutely aware of how much medical knowledge someone needed to care for Paul. This stark reality hit one day as we ate lunch. All the muscles in Paul's face, mouth and throat were very weak. His speech therapist had us take ice and stroke the sides of his face to stimulate a smile, an exercise that helped strengthen his facial muscles.

Apparently his throat muscles were even weaker than we realized. The nurse was feeding Paul small bites of beef when suddenly she realized he was choking. Though we were terrified, Rudy had the presence of mind to grab Paul and perform the Heimlich maneuver to make the beef come up. Iris had the suction machine ready but did not have to use it because Paul cried out in fright, which told us his lungs were clear.

Some days Paul would take one step forward only to take two steps backward the next day. We knew we had to keep up our spirits to help him continue fighting his way back. The Lord was always faithful to strengthen us when we felt we had no more reserves from which to draw. During those difficult days we grabbed for any signs of improvement.

The nurses and therapist worked for weeks trying to teach Paul to push his wheelchair. His muscles were so weak and his coordination so poor that no matter how hard he tried he just could not get it to move. Usually we would put him in it every night after dinner and encourage him to push.

Finally one evening his chair moved ever so slightly. Angie ran and grabbed Paul, saying, "You did it, you did it." We were so thrilled that we called our associate pastor and his wife to come and see what Paul had done. After they came over and saw him move his wheelchair, we had a kitchen full of people laughing, clapping, and crying all at the same time.

Paul was still in diapers, but Rudy and I wanted to let him come back to church as soon as possible. We felt that the love he would receive would encourage him.

Most of our church members had not seen Paul since he was brain damaged, and although they had heard reports about his condition, it was apparent as we entered the church that many of them were not prepared for what they saw. Numerous people came over to speak to us, but others looked straight ahead with tears flowing down their cheeks.

It would take weeks for some people, and months for others, before they could come up and speak to Paul.

The church children had many questions. We tried to carefully answer each one about the wheelchair, the splints on Paul's hands, the casts on his legs, and why he couldn't talk to them. I read the confusion in their eyes. How could this weak little boy be the same Paul they had known all their lives?

Before we set out that first morning for church, we prayed for special strength from the Lord. We knew this day would be hard for our precious friends of many years because they loved Paul dearly. I thought my heart would break as I sat in the pew and watched Rudy get up to preach his first message with Paul sitting there in front of him. I prayed for the Holy Spirit to empower him with strength to finish the message of the morning without breaking down.

The service finally came to a close, and I thanked God for giving us the grace to get through the morning. We prepared to go home, and I noticed Paul's little friends running and playing. As I made my way to the car, the tears started to flow, and I wished with every fiber of my body that Paul could get out of that wheelchair and run and play with them.

The Thanksgiving holiday season was now upon us, but there was no holiday mood at our house. Every family has traditions to celebrate the season and we also had special things that we loved to do each year. We normally had a beautiful meal with Rudy's parents as well as his sisters and their families. Then we would load all the children in the car to go see Santa Claus arrive on a fire engine. We loved to see the excitement on their faces as Santa passed by and threw candy.

This year Rudy and I didn't really have the heart to go, but Angie had looked so forward to going that we went anyway. We knew it was important to keep things as normal as possible for her because there were very few things that had not changed since Paul's illness.

Paul's precious nurse, Iris, and her family were willing to have their Thanksgiving meal at dinner time so we could have our traditional lunch.

The day was hard as we had to work with Paul's cousins to help them understand what a "handicapped" person was and why he couldn't do all the things he used to do. But it was rewarding to see Angie laugh and play, which she hadn't done often during Paul's illness.

Right after Thanksgiving we began to tell Paul the Christmas story about our Savior's birth. We brought out the books we had used years before to teach Angie and Paul the Christmas story, put a small tree in his bedroom, and did everything we could to reinforce what the holiday meant. But on most days when we asked Paul who was born on Christmas day, he just stared at us as though he had never heard of Christmas before.

The Christmas season is our family's favorite time of the year. We love to decorate our home and tree, bake cookies, make candy, go to the church programs, help with the baskets for needy families and generally participate in all of the warmth, beauty and fun of the season. The children always put their special ornaments on the tree and helped decorate the cookies.

To be honest, we did not look forward to the festivities. But once again we knew that we had to try for Angie's sake.

During Christmas week our doorbell rang one night and when I answered it, there stood Santa Claus. We never did know who this precious man was, but we so appreciated him taking an evening from his busy schedule to come and try to brighten our son's holidays. We were not certain Paul understood what the visit was all about, but he enjoyed visiting with the man and pulling at his beard.

People from everywhere sent Paul cards, while others brought gifts for the kids and baked wonderful goodies to show their love for us. Because everyone tried so hard to help us, it gave us the strength to get through those emotionally charged days. Christmas morning tears rolled down our faces as we watched Paul struggle as he was unable to unwrap his gifts. We knew that Christmas might never be the same at our house again.

I don't know how we would have made it through that first Christmas without the love and support of our families. My sister, Barbara, and her family gave up Christmas at their own home to come and be with us. It took a lot of love to load all of the family's gifts in the car and head off to another state. Over the years my sisters and I gave each other so many special gifts, but none could ever be more precious to me than that gift of unselfish love.

CHAPTER 10
The Difficult Winter

As December rolled into January the cold, dark days of winter matched the chill of our spirits.

Rudy and I had such high hopes for Paul's full recovery, but as weeks dragged into months we became more aware that Paul still functioned mentally on the level of a two- or three-year-old at best.

Accepting this reality, we reluctantly relinquished our aspirations and dreams for him and concentrated instead on new directions for him. It was like starting over. Instead of trying to teach him from a third-grade book, we bought large plastic letters and struggled to teach him the alphabet again. Far from watching him throw a basketball through a hoop, we rejoiced over his small victory in squeezing a Nerf ball. This child who had easily spoken or sung at school or church now had to be taught his name and address.

Sharing my personal feelings with others had always been difficult for me. Consequently, most people had no idea of my personal struggle. No matter how hard I cried at home, when I went to church or elsewhere I braced myself and put on a brave smile.

"People expect a pastor's wife to be brave and courageous," I thought. "As a leader in the church, I must set a good example."

How unfortunate for our church members and me! With my brave front I gave them no opening to truly minister to my need. Looking back, I realize how they could not come to me or even share with me their own pain and sorrow because they felt they had to be as brave as I appeared to be. Satan caught me in his web of a false masquerade.

Years later I learned that a major part of the healing process is the freedom to express your fears and pain. I kept all of my grief inside, and as the pain grew I felt more isolated. "No one can understand our pain," I thought.

Slowly I learned that pain is universal; everyone suffers pain and grief at some point in life. Many could understand my hurt, but I needed to open up and let them into my heart.

Support groups were not as prevalent in the early 1980s as they are today. I talked freely to no one except Rudy and my sisters. This meant that Rudy not only had to deal with his own emotions but also lend strength to Angie and me.

Some of Paul's little friends stopped by our house to play games with him. He had not been able to respond and play with them before Christmas, but now he tried Connect Four and Candy Land. On an occasional sunny day we took Paul over to the school at recess time and let him visit with his classmates. The children adapted to this new situation more readily than most adults did. For most of them it was their first exposure to a handicapped person. These school outings proved profitable to Paul as well as his classmates. They wanted to do everything possible for him and asked if they could push his chair or get him a drink.

Our family knew what a courageous little fighter Paul was but we had no idea how much his battle for life had affected others. One night Rudy came home and told me some wonderful news. The gymnasium for our Christian school was nearly complete, and the church and school families wanted to name it in Paul's honor.

Our local newspaper took pictures and published an article about this special event. The gym was packed to capacity on dedication night as we rolled Paul out in his wheelchair to the middle of the gym floor. The plaque in his honor read:

The Paul Holland Gymnasium, in honor of Paul Holland, who has been an inspiration to many with his courageous battle for life and his simple childlike faith in and love for the Lord Jesus Christ. Presented by the members of Berean Baptist Church, January 8, 1982.

Tears of sorrow mixed with joy slipped down my face. In my mind's eye I saw Paul racing up and down the court, fulfilling his dream of playing basketball for his school's team. Now it would take an absolute miracle from God for him to ever do that. But with a rush of joy in my heart I recalled this child's strong testimony of faith in the Lord Jesus during his long illness. Not once had he ever been angry at God for his brain tumor. Instead, he had looked beyond himself to encourage others.

In my heart I knew that God had recorded all of this in Heaven and that Paul would receive his reward at the Judgment Seat of Christ (II Corinthians 5:10). That night we were thrilled beyond measure as all the people in that gym rose to their feet and gave this little soldier of the cross a standing ovation.

In the ensuing weeks Paul became more aware of his surroundings every day. One morning we awoke to that unmistakable hush that indicated snow had fallen during the night. Snow brought out the child in me. I jumped out of bed and rushed to look out and see how deep it was.

Hearing the announcement on the radio about school closings, I hurried to Angie's room to tell her she didn't have to go to school. "After breakfast we'll go out and ride on the sled," I promised.

Snow days were a favorite for our family. After breakfast we wheeled Paul's chair up to the window, and Angie and I threw snowballs in his direction. We took some snow inside and put it in his hand so he could feel how cold it was. We carefully dug out some clean snow and made him some "snow cream." If he couldn't go out to the snow, we would bring the snow in to him!

Most of the time Paul's attempts at bowel and bladder control were still unsuccessful, but we continued to work on this goal hourly. Of course, such control would make it easier to take him out in public. While he was very patient with our efforts, it became obvious this achievement would be a long-term goal.

We watched Paul make great strides in other areas. Through daily physical therapy and home exercises we worked for hours to strengthen his leg muscles so he could walk again. Doctors had told us he lacked muscle strength and nerve impulses to walk, but we saw him progress from struggling to crawl on all four limbs to standing by his bed while holding onto the bed rails.

Finally the doctors gave permission for him to use a walker. Each phase of rehabilitation took months, but he finally stood by himself and, with the walker, took one or two steps.

We constantly wondered what Paul remembered from his life or what he was thinking. We so wished he could express himself. His speech therapist came to the house every day, and Paul did exercises to strengthen his tongue and throat muscles. Up to that point he had said only a few words and never a complete sentence.

One night he lay quietly in bed when the nurse heard him say something. She didn't quite understand so she leaned over to hear his first complete sentence.

"Are you saved?" he asked.

The nurse was deeply moved that Paul's first verbal communication to her was to inquire about her salvation. She assured him that she was indeed saved and could hardly wait until morning to share this accomplishment with us.

Knowing that Paul still understood God's love greatly encouraged us. With his limited abilities he still shared what was of utmost important to him: knowing that others around him had accepted Jesus as personal Savior.

A teacher from our school came to the house to test Paul and assess his mental capacity. The testing took several days since his attention span was brief. The results confirmed our suspicion that he could function only on the level of a two- or three-year-old.

The scores varied widely because his brain was damaged more severely in some areas than in others. Since most of the damage was to the left side of his brain his language abilities were very low. With less right-side brain damage his math skills were more intact.

The teacher devised a curriculum for Paul and we worked every day for short periods of time on math, language developmental skills, colors, shapes, and writing. His short-term memory was minimal, and sometimes we went over the same facts a hundred times before he could recall them.

His fine motor skills were very limited so we played games with him, urging him to grip cards or checkers, forcing him to use those muscles. At first he dropped them almost every time, but we handed them to him again and he would try to hold on. Angie and his little friends loved to play games with him, knowing they were helping with his therapy.

As Paul began to show emotional development he wanted to be where the activity was in the house. When friends came to visit, we sat him right in the middle of the whole group. He had learned a few jokes and, without short-term recall, told them over and over. People were patient, just thankful that he could express himself at all.

Sunday was the highlight of Paul's week. His face lit up during the singing and he said, "I just love gospel music." He didn't seem quite as excited, however, when his dad began to preach. We teased Rudy about his sermons putting Paul to sleep. Actually, Paul often fell asleep when he was still for any length of time, no matter where he was.

Paul continued to beg for food and water because of the pituitary damage. We kept on praying that, in time, he could cope better.

During the month of February Paul's sleep pattern finally began to stabilize, and he slept for at least a few hours at a time. Since he was rarely urinating during the night we asked his doctor if we might care for him by ourselves during the 11-to-7 shift. His doctor was apprehensive, since

Paul could literally dehydrate in a matter of hours if his anti-diuretic hormone was not properly administered, but I assured him that I would set my clock twice a night to check on him. Iris said she would be on call for us in any emergency.

Many people wondered why we wanted to take on this responsibility. Because I had shared most of Paul's care with others for many months, if the doctor felt I could manage even for a few hours at night without registered nurses I wanted that opportunity. We prayed much about this decision and rejoiced when the doctor said, "Let's try it temporarily and see."

Before the change in routine, we took Paul upstairs to see if he recognized his bedroom. He sat down on the bed, looked around and said, "I like this room."

I vividly remember lying down on his bed with him that first night. Again, he shared his favorite jokes with me — the same jokes I had already heard 25 times that day. With his fingers he proudly built the church, the steeple and the people. He again checked me out to be sure I was saved. He hugged me, kissed me and repeatedly said, "I love you."

As we lay there, I knew that no one could ever love him as we did. We willingly sacrificed sleep to get up during the night and have these special times with him. Many nights Rudy, Angie and I would gather on his bed and read to him, play games or just sit there until he fell asleep.

Sometimes when my alarm clock went off in the middle of the night I momentarily wondered why I had set it to go off at such an awful hour. Then the realization would come back to me suddenly — Paul was lying in his bedroom with severe brain damage. Many nights as I slipped into his room to check his diapers, I sat down on the edge of the bed and just cried. In the dark, heavy silence I thought of his efforts to do each task we asked of him. Each day he struggled to master his ABCs, he held tightly to his walker so he could move forward a few steps, and he would invariably say he was sorry when he wet his pants. I was thankful that he was oblivious to all of the things he could do before.

Many times I wondered what the purpose was in all of this. One night as I lay beside Paul on his bed I cried out, "Lord, please help us understand why you allowed all of this to happen."

The Lord impressed on my heart to read I Corinthians 13. I thought, "This is the love chapter of the Bible. I already know what it says. How can I find my answer there?" My emotions were totally distraught as my struggle continued. In my mind I almost screamed, "OK, I will read it even though I know my answer is not there."

Finally I read verse 12. "*For now we see through a glass, darkly; but then face to face: now I know in part; but then shall I know even as also I am known.*" God had given me understanding. His Word revealed to me that while I am on this earth I will never fully know why He had allowed our family to go through this particular valley. Only when we stand before Him face to face will we be able to see it clearly.

"Lord," I prayed, "give me a willing heart to trust You, even when it hurts to the marrow of my bones."

In early March the doctor scheduled an EEG and CAT scan to determine if Paul's tumor was growing back. As we sat in that familiar hall outside the CAT scan area we wondered if the report would be similar to those of 1979 and 1980.

We knew there was nothing else we could do for Paul. He could not have any more surgery or radiation on the tumor.

That evening the radiologist called and said, "The tumor appears dormant at this time." We praised the Lord for the good report.

Those winter months had been long and difficult, but we could look back and see that our diligence had its rewards. Paul had made great strides for a little boy who was supposed to function only in a vegetative state.

CHAPTER 11
Small Things Help

When spring arrived in full bloom its beauty lifted my spirits.

Our home was across the street from a golf course. On sunny winter days, when it was too cold to go outside, Paul would sit at our living room window in his wheelchair and gaze out over the course while soaking in the warmth of the sun. Now it was warm enough to push him on the cart path around the course in late afternoon when there were no golfers playing.

"I just love this," he often said, and I imagined that he felt a sense of freedom among the ponds and trees of that beautiful course that he didn't feel within the four walls of our home.

That spring we had handicapped-adaptable training wheels put on Paul's bicycle to make it steadier and more like a tricycle. We also added straps to keep his feet on the pedals. We hoped he might experience the full joy of riding his bike again, but even with us holding him it was weeks before he could stay on the seat and keep his feet in the straps.

After practicing each day he could finally coordinate the foot motions, and his little face lit up with joy as he realized he was moving forward. Of course, he received the usual round of hugs and kisses for accomplishing a new task. Soon his trips back and forth across our patio on the bicycle, with us running by his side, became a highlight of his day.

Rudy and I love sports, and both of us played on our church's softball teams. We placed Paul's wheelchair at one end of the bleachers, and people came down to visit with him. The stimulation of conversation, coupled with the excitement of the games, always cheered him up. Friends and fun helped.

During his reintroduction to society we had many adventures with Paul. I've always found that humor helped me through difficult times when our only choice was to laugh or cry.

Confined to a wheelchair, Paul had a view of the world that was different from that of someone on his feet. When standing you look at someone at eye level, but not from a wheelchair. When following behind someone, your eye-level view is generally another person's backside.

If we got busy and failed to watch Paul every minute, he became interested in what was in front of him. You have probably guessed what sometimes happened. Whenever someone turned around with a startled look, we knew exactly what part of that person's anatomy Paul had patted.

With all the dignity we could muster and talking as fast as possible, we apologized and explained Paul's brain damage. Everyone responded kindly and we usually laughed together. A sense of humor helps.

One day we took Paul to an amusement park so he could ride around in his wheelchair. We felt he would enjoy all of the sights and sounds. As always, there was a long line to the ladies' bathroom.

"I have to go poo-poo," said Paul.

With his recent switch from diapers to underwear in the daytime, I could only pray that he wouldn't go in his pants. The last few people in front of us in line let us go ahead, and I thought, "Thank God we made it."

I maneuvered Paul into the only available stall, which was not handicapped-accessible. It was extremely crowded. I started pulling his pants down when, all of a sudden, he pooped right on the floor between my feet. I can usually clean up most messes a kid can make but the heat, or the smell, or the cramped conditions in the bathroom made me feel like I would pass out right there.

While I was feeling woozy I forgot to put Paul's urinal in front of him, so he started to wet on me. That finally spurned me into action.

With the Lord's help and about half a roll of toilet paper, I got everything cleaned up.

Sometimes you laugh and cry at the same time.

Paul's sleep patterns stabilized even more and he rested for longer periods at night. This threw him back into his periodic habit of waking up with the chickens most mornings. I got up very early with him, since he had no concept of time and was ready to get up as soon as he awoke, whether it was 5:30 or 8:00 a.m.

We continued to work with him on staying dry during the night and rewarded him each morning when his diapers were dry. Although he worked hard, attainment of this goal would take many more months.

During the summer his teacher stopped his formal school lessons, but we continued school work on a daily basis. Paul enjoyed having Angie home, and she loved helping. She did lessons, played games and exercised with him so he wouldn't feel persecuted.

Everyone we met told us, "We are praying for Paul's recovery and if there is anything we can do to help, please let us know." Most people could not assist us in any way except prayer. However, a man who taught handicapped people to swim asked if he could work with Paul. We considered this a godsend since swimming had once been Paul's favorite pastime.

As a youngster Paul had always been like a fish in the water. He stayed in the pool for hours, always ready to try any new strokes or to jump. One day at the pool he called, "Watch me, Mom," as he jumped off the high-diving board. I held my breath, but he did fine. I was thankful he didn't need my inadequate lifeguard skills.

All summer that devoted man worked with Paul, but we faced the difficult reality that he would never swim as he had before. Rigid and poorly balanced, he found the water frightening. This, too, was a bitter pill to swallow.

One morning a church couple who were like adopted grandparents to Angie and Paul came by for a visit. Paul was gleefully teasing and playing with them when suddenly he froze.

"Paul! Paul!" I screamed. I thought he was dying.

Just as suddenly, he snapped out of it and said, "I feel like I'm going to vomit."

The nurse thought he might be having some seizure activity so we called the doctor, who scheduled an EEG.

Over the next two days I prayed constantly that Paul would not start having seizures again. Each time he had an episode like that I recalled that day in the hospital when they said he couldn't live through the seizures much longer. While the new EEG reading was not conclusive for seizure activity, these episodes continued to increase in frequency throughout the summer.

We wanted to take a family vacation but were afraid to go where we were not familiar with the doctors and hospitals. After praying for guidance we felt we could go to my hometown if a nurse could go with us. Once again, Iris' family gave her up for a week so we could go.

With all of Paul's supplies we looked like we were moving out of our house, but the effort was worth it. Angie had a great time with her cousins — swimming, riding in the boat and trying to ski. The heat kept Paul indoors, but in the cool of the evening we took him on long boat rides. On the water and in the safety of the boat, his little face brightened up like it did when he used to swim.

Those days we spent together, relaxing from all of the tension, helped us keep our sanity. I still have flashbacks of Angie and her cousin Lisa trying to hang onto a bobsled being pulled by the boat. Relaxation and good times helped.

Paul's tenth birthday — August 18, 1982 — was a Wednesday and thus a church night. Our whole church gave him a big birthday party after the service. The gym was gaily decorated and a huge "Dukes of Hazzard" cake and punch were enjoyed. Paul happily ate the cake and opened cards and gifts. Caring friends who showed their love for us were a huge help.

When school opened August 30, we decided to let Paul attend part-time, with two classes for three hours in the morning. September and

October were hard for us as well as his teachers, and we realized that our school simply did not have a place for him. There was no special education program at our Christian school. Teachers and students tried hard, but Paul's medical needs and apparent seizure activity proved too disruptive. One of our hardest decisions was to withdraw Paul from our school, but we knew it was the only fair thing to do for him and the other children.

For Angie's 12th birthday, in late September, she wanted to have her usual sleepover party. Paul's condition was unstable at this time, with his apparent seizure activity getting worse. Rudy and I wondered if, just this once, it would be better not to have a party because Paul's seizures might put a damper on the activities. We broached the subject tactfully but quickly learned that Angie did not favor cancellation.

"Mom, all the kids love Paul," she said. "I'll just explain that he has electrical activity in his brain, making his muscles rigid. They'll understand."

Her party was a great success, especially the shaving cream battle in our backyard. As usual, Paul loved to be in the center of everything, so we sat outside to watch the girls chase each other with shaving cream cans. Since they couldn't squirt shaving cream on Paul, Angie and the girls made him a mustache and beard. It was a wonderful night for both of them.

The wisdom of a child helped.

Every day Paul would grind his teeth, have long bouts of hiccups and vomiting, and definite periods of thrashing his legs and arms. Our worst fear about these episodes was coming true. Paul was having seizures, which became more frequent due to scar tissue developing at the site of the brain trauma.

Rudy and I got very little sleep since one of us was always with Paul during the night to make sure he came out of the seizures. The neurologist put Paul on Tegretol, an anti-convulsant, but he did not tolerate it well because of the side effects.

We felt very fortunate that Paul had never had a seizure in church. Every Sunday I prayed, "Lord, please don't let Paul have a seizure today."

But one Sunday morning a seizure suddenly started. Fear gripped me as I wondered how Rudy could have the grace to stay up in the pulpit and continue to preach.

Rudy stopped abruptly, and all everyone could hear was Paul's seizure. All eyes were riveted on Rudy. I sensed the Holy Spirit strengthening him as he explained to the congregation what was happening to Paul, what seizure activity really was, and that everything would soon be all right since the nurse and his mother knew how to take care of him. The grace of God helped us that morning.

Paul had a grand mal seizure October 29 at 1:15 a.m. We were terrified as we tried to take care of him and call his doctor. The seizure stopped while we were on the phone with the doctor but Paul was motionless and non-responsive. The doctor told us what to do for Paul and also to call Iris in to help care for him. He arranged for an appointment at the hospital to see if another anti-convulsant medication would stop the seizures.

Over the next few months we tried three different medications, none of which were totally successful. During the night I sometimes felt like a jack-in-the-box, constantly jumping up to check on Paul and make sure he was all right. Rudy tried to sleep since he had to work the next day, but I knew he woke up every time I moved.

Many days it was easy to get discouraged. Paul seemed to have eating and drinking on his mind about 90 percent of the time. A special education teacher came to our home, but sometimes Paul appeared totally uninterested in working with her. He did not want to do his exercises or even ride his tricycle.

"What will we do if he never progresses any further?" I wondered.

When he was despondent and unable to cooperate, I felt bitter. Why was sickness all he knew? Why did he have to have seizures? What would we do about school this fall? Would our lives always be like this?

During those difficult days the sermons from the pulpit became more crucial for me. As a pastor's wife I have heard a lot of good preaching, and I probably took it for granted sometimes instead of concentrating fully on the messages. But when you are a needy soul, you listen with a different ear.

"Lord, give me something to help me during this week," I prayed every time I left my house to go to church.

I was afraid that bitterness would take root in my heart as the months wore on. When bitter thoughts assailed, I remembered a visitation night for our church when I met a woman totally consumed with bitterness.

Her daughter had asked us to invite her to church. She had gotten divorced and been angry at her husband and the entire world ever since. I remember the sadness on her daughter's face as she said, "Mom isn't hurting Dad. She's hurting herself and us kids."

That night as we tried to share the love of Christ with her, nothing could break that root of bitterness that had sprung up in her heart. She could see or hear nothing good, since she was consumed by hate. As we rode back to the church that night I prayed, "Lord, don't ever let me become so bitter that I can't feel love anymore."

As I sat under the preached Word, my heart was like a dry desert that needed to be watered by the showers of God's love. The preached Word helped keep the seed of bitterness from taking root.

CHAPTER 12
The Hospital Trial

Over the next few months we devoted a lot of time and effort to learning how special education worked within the public school system.

Placement of a child within the program is done through a battery of tests and evaluations by different professionals. Rudy and I met with the director of special education as well as principals, teachers, doctors and psychologists to formulate an individualized education plan. This plan is required for each special-needs child since goals and needs vary widely. Paul's progress could be measured through this plan.

For the remainder of the 1982-83 school year, homebound special education teachers were provided for Paul due to his frequent seizure activity in the classroom. This program met with only limited success.

The next year he was placed in a regular school with one-on-one instruction. Paul showed small amounts of progress but he did not like school as he had before. We were deeply concerned about finding a program that would meet his educational needs and allow him to thrive socially. We thought that the isolation from other children in the one-on-one program might be the source of his unhappiness with school.

After many more meetings it was determined that placement the next year would be in a multi-handicapped class. Of course, Paul's nurse would have to accompany him to meet his medical needs, but she would sit where he could not see her, to encourage his independence. Our ultimate goal was for Paul to mesh with the other children.

Any transition was extremely hard for him and all of these changes were no exception. Yet we began to see improvements and feel that he was finally in the program best suited to his needs. During that time Rudy and I attended multiple meetings at school to address Paul's individualized Education Plan. All of the school staff worked diligently to formulate the best plan.

From a medical standpoint, Paul's seizures proved extremely difficult to manage. His physician tried many individual drugs and combinations of anti-convulsant drugs in an attempt to control them. Some dosages made him too sleepy, while other proved toxic and caused him to vomit. He suffered strong complex seizures day and night.

The doctors told us that Paul did not suffer during the seizures, but watching him endure them almost tore out our hearts. We prayed constantly that God would give the doctors wisdom to deal with this monumental problem. After another hospitalization and consultation with a seizure specialist from Germany who was working at the University of Virginia for a year, the seizure activity got somewhat better.

The doctors explained that the dosage required to completely stop the seizures would make Paul sleep most of the time. The other option was to have him coherent but with some seizure activity. While neither choice was ideal, we chose to live with the seizures so that Paul would have some semblance of a normal life.

Our family was being affected tremendously at this time by Paul's long illness and the constant seizures. Angie began to have problems during that school year. Her grades dropped and she wanted to stay home all the time. We tried to reassure her that everything humanly possible was being done to care for Paul, yet I knew she feared he might not survive. This fear also triggered thoughts that her father or I might die.

Years later she told us of the feelings that tormented her during this time. When we had to leave the house, she would run to the window and watch for us to drive back into the driveway. She cried with fear that something might happen to us. She hid these feelings from us because she understood our concern for Paul.

Angie also developed constant stomach pain and we worked with her pediatrician to see if she had developed an ulcer or other gastrointestinal problems. Nothing showed up on the tests, and the doctor said she was reacting psychologically to all of the stress of Paul's illness. Rudy and I spent a lot of time working her through these fears, trying to put Paul's illness into proper perspective for her.

During this period Angie also desperately wanted us to have another child. Rudy and I love kids and had wanted four children. Our plans were to have two more when Angie and Paul were both in school. Of course, Paul's problems started around that time so we delayed, fervently seeking God's direction. We spent many nights discussing the pros and cons of having a baby.

On one hand, we certainly wanted another child, but we wondered how we could take care of a baby and Paul at the same time. We were getting up 6-8 times a night with Paul's seizures. Ultimately, our heart-wrenching decision was that having additional children would not be in our family's best interests. Angie found this extremely hard to understand as she had little idea of the true extent of Paul's care.

As I explained earlier, Angie inherited a stubborn streak from her parents. She announced one day that if we would not have another child, she would pray for God to give us one to adopt. We tried to explain that you had to take care of an adopted child also, but that did not deter her fervent prayers for a brother or sister. Her childlike faith that God is bigger than circumstances was rewarded.

One of my sisters had gone through a difficult divorce and remarried. My niece, Melanie, was extremely unhappy in her new step-family environment. Our families are close, and she called to ask us if she could come live with us.

The first time she called Paul was so sick that I knew we would not have the time to care for him and help her with all of the problems she was dealing with at that time. Sadly, we had to tell her that she couldn't come but we promised that if we could get Paul stabilized enough we would consider it the next year. Meanwhile, Angie continued to pray for us to adopt a child.

In the summer of 1984 we talked at great length to my sister and to Melanie and Angie about Melanie coming to live with us. Everyone thought we were crazy to even consider taking on additional responsibilities. Yet, with Melanie's unhappiness at home we feared that she might rebel and get into a detrimental lifestyle unless we intervened.

When we told Angie that Melanie was coming to live with us she said, "I told you God would give me a brother or sister." Childlike faith helped.

God's Word teaches that it is more blessed to give than to receive, and He proved faithful to His Word. As we helped Melanie, God provided the answer to Angie's fears. We saw those fears begin to disappear as Angie and Melanie spent time together amid the activities of normal 14-year-old girls. What neither we nor the doctors had been able to do, God did through our willingness to help others in need.

Many times people asked us to let Paul get up in church and say verses or sing. Rudy and I have always been totally sold out to sharing the love of Christ in any way possible, but we knew that Paul did not know what was appropriate to say in church. We also felt that if he had a seizure while in front of the congregation it would totally disrupt the service. We made the difficult decision for Rudy or me to share Paul's story instead of allowing him to participate directly.

On two different occasions we heard preachers say that Paul would be a blessing to their congregations. "Please let Paul quote a verse or sing," they said. Twice we let Paul try to do this.

The first time he kept hitting the microphone as the preacher tried to ask him questions. The second time he quoted John 3:16 and sang "Jesus Loves Me." Just as I said to myself, "Thank you God, he did OK," Paul broke out in another song — "Hey Good Lookin.'"

We felt it was best for Paul to share one-on-one in the future.

When Paul went back to school from the homebound program I suddenly found myself lost. For three years almost all of my time had been devoted to Paul's rehabilitation program. Now, with everyone gone during the day, the house seemed so big and quiet. My thoughts were constantly on Paul's school program, his seizures and his prognosis.

One day Rudy and I had lunch with a gentleman who owned a computer sales company. We discussed, among other things, my background in office management. Suddenly he asked if I would be interested in coming to work as his office manager.

Working outside the home had not entered my mind for three years. I told him I would consider it, never seriously thinking that I might take the job. But to honor my promise, Rudy and I prayed about it that night. The money would certainly come in handy to pay off some of the medical bills, and Rudy felt the change might be good for me. Two days later I called the man back and told him I would give it a try.

Learning about computers intrigued me, and soon my boss asked if I would also become a software support representative, going out and training employees to use their new computers and software. Again, God knew what was best for me. The stimulation of learning and working with others to use their computers proved to be good for me mentally, and I was able to fill my mind with productive thoughts instead of just fearful ones.

Paul's progress at school in the fall of 1984 was promising. His class had received a new computer with programs designed especially for mentally handicapped children.

Writing was so difficult for Paul since his surgery, but the computer gave him the freedom to do math without having to write, and this became his favorite subject. The area of the brain that handles math was not as severely damaged as the part that handles language, so Paul could comprehend math much more readily.

Paul's three-month physical exam was scheduled for late September. After the physical the neurologist discussed placing Paul in a highly successful rehabilitation hospital about a four-hour drive from home. He felt that Paul had not shown substantial improvement. He continued to experience seizure activity, but with the programs and therapists that this hospital could provide he could possibly show additional improvement.

My idea of any mental hospital was drawn from what I had read and seen in movies. All I could think of was Paul sitting somewhere in a corner all drugged up so that he wouldn't bother anyone, or worse — that someone might physically or sexually abuse him. Paul was totally dependent upon others for his care and could not fend for himself. Would they take good care of him? How would I know if anyone was hurting him in any way?

Our family was fiercely protective of Paul, but we deeply respected his physician's recommendations. The doctor could tell that we were appalled by such a proposal, but we told him we would visit the facility and pray about it.

When we got into the car that day I thought, "No way can I let Paul go away to a hospital." For days I could not even bring myself to pray about it, but then the hospital called to see if we could come for a visit. This forced us to seek God's will about hospital placement even though my heart and mind didn't cooperate very readily.

On the morning we drove up, I was certain we would not like it, but as we entered the property I could see that it had beautiful facilities. Our appointment with the doctor lasted more than an hour as he explained how a rehabilitation program was designed for each child. The staff included doctors, psychologists and nurses, as well as physical, occupational and recreational therapists. Each bright, cheerful room housed two children to allow for social interaction. As we toured the facility we saw that the children were busy and seemed happy.

The hospital would be ready to accept another child in two weeks and they would let us know in a few days if they felt that Paul would fit into their program. They asked us to use this time to consider if we felt that hospital placement was appropriate for Paul.

I agonized over the next few days about entrusting Paul's care to someone else completely. "Would they be good to him?" I wondered. "Would he be happy?"

Each time the phone rang I feared it was hospital saying they felt Paul could come. When the call finally came, I spent the rest of the day crying. We felt that we had to give it a try if all of the professionals thought Paul would benefit from the program.

The hospital had a toll-free number we could call each morning and evening to get a report on Paul. There was also a dormitory-type building where we could stay when we came to visit.

Those six months he spent there were among the most difficult our family went through during Paul's illness. We worked all week until Friday at noon, went home to pack, and picked up Angie and Melanie at 3:00 p.m. to go to the hospital. Friday evening and most of Saturday were spent with Paul, playing games with him and going to any activities the hospital had planned.

We had to drive home Saturday evening after dinner because Rudy had to preach Sunday morning. Every time we drove away there were tears, and no one was able to say anything for a while.

That fall was also when Rudy's father was diagnosed with lung cancer. Although he underwent chemotherapy, he was gravely ill within just a few months. During the week we would spend as much time as possible with him — at first in the hospital, then at home, and finally in a hospice. Sometimes as we drove back and forth I wondered how Rudy could bear to see his dad so ill while his son was away at a rehabilitation hospital. I constantly prayed for God to strengthen Rudy during those months, especially the day of his dad's funeral.

Paul's six-month stay ended in April of 1985, and we brought him home with great expectations for marked improvement.

After a transition period of about a month, the neurologist ordered a new battery of tests for an updated evaluation. We were deeply disappointed to find that, in spite of the fine programs at the hospital, Paul had regressed as much as two years on some levels. The conclusion was that Paul did, in fact, thrive best in a loving home environment.

Rudy and I still do not understand exactly why God directed us to let Paul go to the hospital; that is another question to be answered when we get to Heaven. But we can rest in the assurance that our child does best when he is at home with us, even though we had to give him every chance for as much progress as possible.

CHAPTER 13
Angie's Decision

In the summer of 1985 Angie had a very complicated maxillofacial surgery to correct some bone deformities in her face. The orthodontist had worked for more than six years with braces to get her teeth in place for maxillofacial surgery. Her mouth was wired together for eight weeks after the operation.

Since she could not eat solid foods she lost weight quickly — down to 89 pounds — and was constantly in need of some kind of nourishment. Between caring for Paul and always pureeing some type of food for Angie, there were many times that summer I thought I would drop from exhaustion.

We also had to deal with the mental aspects of Angie's continual hunger and severe weight loss. Eighty-nine pounds was not an ideal weight for a self-conscious 14-year-old girl. But the wires finally came off, and Angie soon put on weight. God's promises of strength for the journey were precious to me that summer.

In the fall, Rudy began to pick up every virus or cold that came along. This was extremely unusual because he was never sick. In November the doctor finally put him in the hospital with one particular virus that persistently hung on.

Our doctor told Rudy that he just had to get more rest, but we wondered how in the world he could do that. He worked long, hard hours handling his pastoral responsibilities and tried to take turns getting up with Paul during the night. I was working full-time to help with the medical bills in addition to caring for Paul and the girls and managing the house. Rudy and I always tried to go to all of the girls' games and other activities. We felt it was important to support their involvement in school and church so they would not be tempted to choose detrimental activities.

We sought God's direction in how to rearrange our schedules since there weren't many responsibilities we could actually give up. We began alternating nights getting up whenever Paul had a seizure, hoping that some full nights of sleep would help. After four years the lack of sleep was taking its toll on both of us.

I was having frequent stomach trouble from the stress. Another adjustment we made was getting someone to come in and clean the house. God gave us a precious lady from our church that came one day a week to help with the cleaning. Rudy and I also talked to Angie and Melanie and explained that sometimes only one of us might be at their activities.

Everyone in the family had to make adjustments to meet the demands of caring for Paul. Rudy and I were so proud of the way Angie and Melanie rallied to be understanding and help in any way they could.

Although both of them went to school, worked part-time jobs and were actively involved in school and church functions, they tried to find ways to help. They worked at keeping their bedroom and bathroom clean and helped with the dinner dishes. We all wanted to keep Paul at home, so each of us was willing to give up some things and/or take on new responsibilities to keep him with us.

In many ways Angie and Melanie had to act mature beyond their years. It is often difficult for teenagers to constantly put someone else's needs ahead of their own. Rudy and I always tried to show appreciation to the girls for how they pitched in and helped, because we didn't want to take their efforts for granted.

Melanie worked hard during high school to become a good athlete. She wanted to coach as a career, so she played volleyball, basketball and softball for the experience.

As team captain during her senior year she reached beyond herself to encourage the younger players on her team. From the bleachers we often heard such words as, "Come on, you can do it. Just give it your best." That was like an echo of the words Rudy and I had said to her when she came to us as an insecure 14-year-old.

Special Olympics is a wonderful program for special-needs people. Many of the events are handicapped-accessible. Through his school Paul practiced and practiced to participate in the softball throw and bowling events.

We all looked forward with anticipation to the Saturday of the games. By nature I am tender-hearted toward any children but even more so toward handicapped children. As we marched in the parade around that field, I felt my heart would burst with pride for these special people.

Each athlete pushed to succeed in his or her particular events — often with braces, a walker or in a wheelchair. A beautiful smile crossed the face of every one who stepped onto the stand to receive a medal. Rudy and I were deeply touched, but we had no idea how impressed Angie was with these athletes until she came to us one night with an announcement.

She shared with us her deep respect for these Special Olympians who gave their best even if they could not always win. After praying for several years seeking God's direction for her life with regard to her vocation, she determined that she would work with mentally handicapped people.

As I sat across from her and saw her face glow as she told about the peace God had given her with this decision, my mind drifted back to my own surrender to God's calling upon my life when I was 16 years old. I was so thankful that I had surrendered to His will that night. Though our family had gone through many deep valleys, I knew we could have no greater blessing than a child who loved the Lord and wanted His will in her life. God is truly faithful.

I had changed jobs and was working as a personnel consultant help-ing companies locate the right people for whatever positions they might have open. Many times a client would come in either unhappy in a present job or because of a layoff. I was able to encourage them to rise above their circumstances because I understood what it was like to get knocked down and have to pick yourself up again. God allowed me to reach out to others and share what He had taught us.

In the summer of 1986 Angie had additional reconstructive surgery on her face. Her jaws were wired shut again, but she could at least eat soft food after six weeks. We sometimes felt we were trying to support the local hospital single-handedly.

Paul had an MRI scan in February of 1987 to check on the tumor. Even though we knew these tests were essential to be sure the tumor was still dormant, we always faced them with a lot of apprehension. All of the "what ifs" as Rudy called them, went through my mind. In the weeks before the scan I would ask questions like, "What will we do if the tumor is growing back?"

Paul had to be sedated since he couldn't sit still long enough for them to administer the test. We got a good report for which we were thankful. It seemed hard to believe Paul had been sick for six years.

Angie got permission from her own principal as well as the principal at Paul's school to visit in his class occasionally. She had opportunities to help a student from time to time. The specific task didn't matter to Angie — she just loved working with these children. Rudy and I felt the exposure she received in an actual classroom situation was invaluable. She also worked in and later taught a special education Sunday school class at our church, and her eyes would light up when she told us about the different children she met. The bond she had with Paul was incredible, and she was determined to be a part of his life.

Paul continued in his special education program which included light academic work, home living skills and workshop assignments. He also had either speech or physical therapy every day. In spite of the constant night seizures and occasional day seizures he struggled to do all the tasks asked of him.

As we saw the girls begin to mature into young women, I thanked God for giving us the strength to go on. Many mornings when the clock would go off, we would be so tired from working all day and getting up all during the night with Paul. Rudy or I would whisper, "I don't think I can get up this morning and face all the responsibilities of another day." But we both had learned that successful living sometimes was just having the courage to put your foot on the floor and face the day with whatever it brought.

Many mornings as I lay there I thanked God for giving me a husband who was also my best friend to travel this road with me. Rudy had been such a source of strength for all of us over the years. When I thought of God's plan for the man at the head of the family, I wondered how Rudy had been able to be husband, father and Uncle Rudy while also being pastor of our church.

CHAPTER 14
Years of Change

Graduation from high school for Angie and Melanie was June 5, 1988. My sister and her family came for the weekend graduation exercises. We wondered repeatedly where all the years had gone as we shared this special occasion. I remembered my mother talking about how quickly children grow up, and her words were certainly true on this day. As we helped the girls with their caps and gowns, I felt so proud of both of them for all they had accomplished over the last four years.

After the ceremony we had a beautiful party for the girls with family, church members and friends invited. In the quiet of the night, long after the festivities ended, I felt a twinge of sadness. I finally woke Rudy and asked him if it had bothered him during the day to realize that Paul would never graduate from high school and go off to college. He said that thought had been in the back of his mind also. Paul had been sick for nine years at this point, but there were still times when it was tough to turn loose former dreams and aspirations for him. We cried a little together that night before falling back to sleep.

The second love of our life, our church, was going through some financial difficulties at this time. We gave all of our available financial assets to help the church, and after much prayer, we decided to sell our home and give the equity as well. I felt good about our decision, although it was hard to leave our home filled with so many memories of birthday parties, church youth group outings, and just day-to-day living with our children.

August was a busy month with Paul's 16th birthday and the girls getting ready to leave for college. Angie was going to Tennessee Temple University in Chattanooga to study for a degree in special education, while Melanie was leaving for Florida and Clearwater Christian College to major in physical education. Both of the girls loved working with kids, and we felt good about their career choices. But I don't think any of us were truly prepared for how hard it would be.

Melanie called home in the first few weeks crying, "There's a snake out in the hall!" Rudy tried to calm her down enough to have her call the Maintenance Department. He assured her there was nothing he could do from 800 miles away.

Angie got off on a rough foot also. During her first week it rained every day and her roommate was sick. One night Angie took her to the doctor and upon returning to the dorm was flashed by a man wearing a raincoat and nothing else. She ran to her room and called home crying hysterically. We had to calm her down so she could tell her dorm parents and have them call security.

Rudy was faced with a terrible dilemma — Melanie crying in Florida, Angie crying in Tennessee, and me in Roanoke begging him to let them come home. Although we can laugh about it now, it was quite a feat to keep them in school that first month.

Paul settled into another school year and joined the handicapped bowling league. He had such a good time with a handicapped-adaptable ramp to hold the ball.

He had a 24-hour EEG in February of 1989 to monitor seizure activity. The report showed considerable seizure activity throughout sleep so his Dilantin was increased in an effort to reduce the frequency of night seizures. We also placed Paul on the Feingold diet which is mostly natural foods free of additives and preservatives.

The combination of increased medication and dietary changes led to some reduction in seizure activity. Paul's doctor ordered another MRI that showed the tumor still present but dormant. We praised God for these answers to our prayers.

That month also saw the final home game of the season for the Berean Christian Academy basketball team. Angie and her boyfriend came home from college for the weekend, and they went to the game with us.

At the end of the junior varsity game Paul's nurse, Mary Ann, told me he needed to go to the bathroom. Just when I started wondering when they were coming back the school principal made a special announcement — the school and the team dedicated this final game to Paul.

At that moment Paul came walking out onto the floor, assisted by Mary Ann, his nurse, dressed in a Berean Christian Academy basketball uniform. There was hardly a dry eye in the house as everyone gave him a standing ovation.

As he sat on the bench with the team during the first half of the game, my mind drifted back to the night the gym was dedicated and I remembered how desperately Paul had wanted to play on the basketball team. I don't think anyone could ever know how much we appreciated them giving this night to Paul and our family.

At the close of that school year, Melanie moved back to Tennessee so she could be close to her family while continuing her education. Although we missed having her with us, we felt she had made the right decision.

With the continuing difficulties at the church, Rudy felt impressed of the Lord to resign our ministry at Berean Baptist Church. He felt God had closed the door to his pastorate there and was now calling him to a ministry of evangelism and encouragement. After 19 years of ministry we resigned our church June 11, 1989.

Rudy and I took a three-day vacation and launched Rudy Holland Ministries on June 17th with Pastor George Riddell of Williamstown, New Jersey. Rudy is a soul winner and preacher first and foremost, but so often during Paul's illness various churches had wanted Rudy to come and speak on how our family had dealt with the challenges from a Christian perspective. Rudy had never felt he could be away from our church to travel and speak on this subject, but he would now have the freedom to tour and share the lessons God had taught us.

Paul, Angie and I traveled with Rudy whenever possible that summer. Angie has a lovely singing voice and often would sing in the services. We loved ministering in different churches, seeing lost people saved and hurting people encouraged by our message.

Everywhere we went we met people struggling with personal tragedies — a loss of a job, financial security, health problems, divorce or even death. They all needed encouragement.

Since we couldn't go everywhere, we made a video entitled "Five Lessons I've Learned From Tragedy" and shared it with people as well. The response was immediate and phenomenal. We started receiving letters from people who had watched the video and were encouraged by the message.

Many times we do not understand the workings of God in our lives. Leaving our church had been extremely difficult for us, but we began to see that God had another work for us at this point in our lives.

With fall approaching, we had to come to a decision about Paul and me continuing to travel with Rudy. In 22 years of marriage Rudy and I were fortunate in that we had not spent many nights apart, and I knew adjusting to his long absences from home would be extremely difficult for Paul and me. Plus, Angie would be leaving for college at the same time.

I would not only have to deal with the loneliness but also the total care of Paul except for the few hours we still had a nurse. That meant I would have to get up night after night, without relief, with Paul having seizures.

We knew Paul did best in familiar surroundings with a regular schedule. We just felt it would be too difficult for him to be constantly on the road. Angie returned to Tennessee Temple for her sophomore year and Rudy started a heavy fall schedule.

About this same time we received notice from our insurance company that it would no longer pay for Paul's nursing care. We were confident they could not take this action since our doctor prescribed the nurses and our contract provided for this service. We made several appeals with different people at the insurance company, but to no avail.

We felt our only recourse was to sue the insurance company for breach of contract. We had such confidence we would win the case that we kept Paul's nurse employed at our own expense and had borrowed thousands of dollars by the time the case got to court. Unfortunately, the judge ruled in favor of the insurance company because of a law of which we were totally unaware. We had continued our insurance coverage through the church under the COBRA laws, but we found out that churches have no protection under COBRA, so we had no coverage and no case.

It was a dark day when our attorney called with the ruling. How could we pay back all of that money? How could I care for Paul around the clock with no help? He still required constant care. We had been through many trials, but I felt there was no way I could hold up under this.

On April 13, 1990, we had to say goodbye to Paul's wonderful nurse, Iris Dacal Teijeiro. She had worked faithfully to bring Paul from a vegetative state to a point far beyond what anyone predicted to be possible. We embraced and cried the day she left. How do you sufficiently say, "Thank you," to someone who had served so far beyond the call of duty? I know she will have a reward in Heaven for her faithful service to one of God's special children.

The school system provided an aide to care for Paul's needs so that he could continue in school. I was terrified to trust him to an untrained person but God gave us a wonderful Christian lady as an aide. She had a mentally handicapped family member herself, and her degree was in special education.

We spent many hours on the phone and both of us prayed heavily before she accepted the job with Paul. From her own family's experiences she understood my fears. I accompanied her to school until I was confident she understood how to administer Paul's medication. Once again, God provided just the right person at the right time.

Many of our friends banded together to pray for special strength for me during those months until Angie and/or Rudy could be home. God met the need as always. When I thought I could go no farther, Paul would have a couple of nights without seizures and I could get some badly needed rest.

Paul and Angie finished school in June of 1990 and we hit the road again, traveling from coast to coast. We were captivated by the beauty of the United States from Lancaster County, Pennsylvania to San Francisco, California. God allowed us to minister in big churches, small churches, a youth camp, and one-on-one. What a blessing to meet and work with so many Christians who needed encouragement.

Angie returned to college in the fall for her junior year. When she left my heart was heavy as I thought that Paul would probably be leaving with her for his first year of college had it not been for the brain tumor. I cried again that day, but knew that life must go on.

Angie would try to come home as often as possible on the weekends to help with Paul. I would often hear Angie and Paul laughing and teasing with each other. Paul just loved all the attention she gave him, and he would quote Bible verses and sing.

Paul was a constant source of wonderment to me. Many times I wondered how pleasant it would be to live on this earth and not have to deal with any of the evil that is such a real part of the world. This kind of life was true for Paul — he was totally uninhibited by so much that binds us in our relationships with God and other people. When he prayed before a meal he was not concerned with the hustle and bustle of the day. After thanking God for the food he took the time to tell Jesus how much he loved Him.

When Paul saw someone who was sick or hurting, he didn't promise to pray for that person sometime in the future. Again unaware of time or who might be around, he would take their hand, bow his head and ask God to help that person.

One of the most beautiful sights God allowed us to see was when we glimpsed real love through Paul's life. Sometimes when I would struggle to get him in and out of the tub or put on his shoes and braces, he would pat me on the arm and say, "Mom, I love you because you take such good care of me." Often I would hear him tell a teacher or nurse, "I love you because you have been so good to me."

Most precious was his eagerness to share his love with his Savior. He would frequently tell us, "When I get to Heaven I am going to say, 'Thank you Jesus for helping me to eat, sleep, walk and talk. I just love you.'"

You can see how blessed and honored we were to have one of God's choicest servants living in our home. He was truly an open Bible.

Rudy completed his first year of evangelism and encouragement in June of 1990 after speaking in more than 66 churches. We saw many people come to know Christ as Savior and others grow in their walk with Him. We continued via mail or telephone to work with families who needed encouragement.

I have been amazed to see God's direction in our lives. When I surrendered my life to God's call almost 30 years ago I would never have dreamed what kind of direction it would take.

I acquired a new desire to minister to people who are sick, working either with children or cancer patients. While running the ministry office and caring for Paul, I began going to college part-time to become a registered nurse. I knew it was a long-term goal but, even if I didn't complete my studies, I would be able to use everything I learned to be more proficient in caring for Paul without other nursing help.

CHAPTER 15
Learning to Move Forward

*I*n retrospect, 20 years later, Rudy and I wanted to share more with you about how God sustained us to care for Paul as he suffered the ravages of his brain tumor.

When we left Berean, I was totally devastated. Within a matter of months, Rudy resigned; we went through personal bankruptcy; and we lost everything. He had pledged all our assets as collateral on loans for the church.

Once he resigned, we felt lost for a time. These were our best friends, people with whom we had reared our children. Angie and Paul were born while we were at Berean; these folks had gone through Paul's illness with us. Our lives were so intertwined. They were our prayer partners, our encouragers, virtually our entire social network.

Our last big event at our home was a graduation party for Angie and Melanie. This celebration was so important to Rudy and me for them. I remember how much we did not want them to be affected by what was happening to us. I felt like I was dying inside while I was planning this great celebration. From a mom's perspective, you think about all of the milestones in a family's life and how you want to validate your children's efforts and accomplishments.

We struggled to make it a time of rejoicing but inside we were heart-broken at the thought of resigning our beloved church.

We were so "local church" oriented that I think God had to close the door or we would have been at Berean to this day. Looking back, I didn't sense God's hand in it all as much because I was too focused on my own hurt at leaving all that was familiar to us.

A lot had changed from the late 1970s when we had been one of the fastest-growing churches in the state of Virginia. Of course, it started when Paul first got sick, and we essentially brought him home to die. The emotional and financial strain was horrific, as was the toil of trying to keep life normal for Angie. The physical problems she had included several maxillofacial surgeries where her mouth would be wired together for weeks. Many times Rudy and I stayed up all night talking and asking God why all this was happening. It almost seemed we went from one crisis to the next.

Rudy often took the macho attitude of, "We can handle it." He did that in front of others, yet when he was alone he had the same fears I did.

When you are in leadership and you have to divide your focus, you are destined for some problems. If you have to take on too many other responsibilities, for whatever reason, you cannot function at the same level of productivity.

Someone said shortly before we left that Rudy wasn't winning souls like he used to. In the early years of our church, Rudy went visiting every Monday night, Tuesday night, Thursday night and Saturday morning. In the later years Rudy was coming home and getting on his knees with the nurse trying to teach our son to crawl, or to spend time with Angie and me in our moments of despair. He wasn't the young, sharp, full-of-energy guy he used to be. He had been hit in the gut.

I think if you have to go through these types of catastrophic situations and think that things are going to stay the same, you're being unrealistic. Circumstances are going to change whether you want them to or not. Rudy could no longer function in the same way he had before Paul's illness; that's what seemed so hard for some people to grasp.

The church had been in a building program during the Carter administration when the economy produced double-digit inflation and double-digit interest rates. A storm blew down a portion of the new building, and the church leadership had to start over with new financing at those higher rates. All of this was happening at church while Rudy juggled the finances of our own family as well because of Paul's catastrophic illness.

Having all the demands of a large church, school ministry, and now building program debt with a double-digit interest rate on you at one time, plus extreme family sickness on top of everything else in life, can produce moments of sheer terror. Knowing that your child is helpless and must be cared for 24 hours a day, in combination with all the church issues and our gut-level desire to make it all work, was staggering. You feel like you are running as fast as you can but are getting further and further behind.

Since we have been in several churches, I can see what a different experience it is to birth a church like we did at Berean. The sense of responsibility is so much stronger when you were there from the very beginning.

When you go to a place where no one knows you, as we did when Rudy was 23 and I was 22 — well, I am amazed sometimes that we were actually brave enough to do it. I was pregnant with Angie. We had no congregation, and no support. We just went with a desire in our heart to do what we felt God wanted us to do.

We started the church in a restaurant and moved to a radio station. We purchased land and built a building. We were so intricately involved in all of it.

When you start every program, and see so many people saved, many of whom you led to Christ yourself, and you minister to them and their children, performing their weddings and funerals, to leave that much of your life's work and just walk away feels like tearing out a piece of your heart.

When Rudy sensed God leading him to resign at Berean, he took three days in the mountains to pray and seek guidance about this life-changing decision. Leaving this ministry and going into evangelism was one of the most difficult decisions we have ever made. However, after his time alone with God in the mountains, he felt that was the call of God for our lives.

It didn't take long, however, for me to become aware of all the ramifications of our resignation. There was no more salary, and Paul's insurance would be carried for only 30 days.

We had lost our case with the insurance company regarding his coverage because churches were not covered under COBRA laws. What company would want to take on a case like Paul's? The only thing that saved us was that we got new insurance before our group coverage lapsed and were therefore covered for pre-existing conditions.

We lost our support system, our church, our salary, our insurance, our home — everything!

Although Paul was now 18 years old, he was not an adult male in the physical sense and never would be. We gave him growth hormones from age seven to nine to help him maintain his natural development, but after he lost his mental abilities we decided not to continue.

Because he no longer received testosterone, he had no facial hair or sexual development as he grew older. We knew that sexual development would only bring problems through desires and needs that he couldn't understand. In addition, as Paul grew taller and heavier, it would be much harder for us to handle him safely. His actual weight was about 110 pounds, which made it possible for us to keep him safe during his many seizures.

Our endocrinologist, Dr. Blizzard, was one of the foremost experts on growth hormone science in the world. He was the one who suggested that we take these measures.

"If it was your child, would you give him testosterone?" Rudy asked.

"No," said the doctor. "Paul will never father children or become sexually active. Why would you want to create desires in him that would just cause problems, not to mention all of the additional work from such tasks as shaving and caring for him as a grown man?"

We never had to take anything away from Paul. We just chose not to give him certain things that were available, such as synthetic hormones.

This decision was made nearly 30 years ago, when it was still a revolutionary idea in medical science.

Since Paul was not yet 21, he could still go to school. A developmentally disabled person is considered eligible for the purposes of federally-mandated education until the age of 21.

As long as the child is a minor, the value of his or her assets is based on the parents. It's easy to be caught in the middle where you are not strong enough financially to take care of all the medical bills yourself but not poor enough to get help from the government.

That was one of the paradoxical problems we faced. It took everything two people could make to keep Paul going, so there were extreme financial pressures in addition to everything else. There was little aid available because our assets had to count as his assets.

A big turning point for us was when he could qualify for SSI (Supplemental Security Income) at age 18. He would get a small check or about $450 per month, but more importantly was the fact that he got a Medicaid card that allowed him to get prescription drugs for a small co-pay in most cases.

Medicaid also helped in other ways. When Paul was younger and had longer hospital stays, Rudy would have to come up with large sums of money and then file a claim with the insurance company. Many times, without my knowledge, he would go to the bank and get a 90-day note for $25,000 or so, and get reimbursed later. That kind of financial pressure was there all the time, until Medicaid took over when Paul turned 18 years of age.

From 18 to 21 we still had some outside care. He could go to school, for instance, and have someone go with him to provide one-on-one assistance. One lady who went to school with him was a former teacher, a pastor's wife, and just a wonderful person.

Because of this assistance I was able to go back to school part-time. It also allowed us enough help that Angie could peacefully return to college, and Rudy could stay in the ministry.

It was so very important for us to make our abnormal circumstances normal so our lives could move forward in God's plan. We just knew that, with God's help, we could do it.

In time, we realized that Paul could live for a very long time in this condition — perhaps even outliving us — and we had to prepare for that. We talked to our attorney and made provisions for him in case something happened to us.

When we started this process, Paul was on Medicaid which covered most of his medical bills. We could set up a trust fund provided through a life insurance policy on Rudy that Angie could use to take care of his other needs.

As the parents of a developmentally disabled child, we were so afraid that someone would do something to hurt him and he couldn't tell us. That made us afraid to leave him in almost any environment outside of our own home.

We talked to Angie about this and we looked at it from both sides, as Paul's parents and as Angie's parents. Ideally, from Paul's perspective, we would love for Angie to be in charge of looking after him if something happened to us. But we also knew what challenges we have gone through as his parents and to ask a sibling to assume this responsibility was a huge commitment. She adored Paul just as we did, but we knew that one day she would marry a man who had not known Paul but for a short time and didn't have that same bond. We knew Angie wanted to do this, but would assuming that responsibility be fair to her? Realistically, we felt her future family would have to be considered. So we thought that if she had appropriate financial reserves, she could provide the best care for Paul while taking care of her own family as well.

Rudy took out an extremely large life insurance policy on himself to provide in case we were both deceased, so that the money would be available and last long enough. We also drew up the appropriate wills and trust agreements to make certain the funds were distributed correctly. We had a family agreement with Angie that this trust fund would be used to take care of Paul.

I had often heard the saying, "God always gives special children to special people." That sounds great on a greeting card but it's not true.

It's not uncommon for special-needs children to be abandoned by at least one parent. In most cases it is the father. The first social worker assigned to us in Virginia many years ago told us that 80 to 90 percent of couples in these situations ultimately divorce because of the pressure.

People forget that in these situations everything else goes on. Your bills, the demands of full-time jobs, the needs of your other children, and ordinary pressures of family life — none of that stops. In our case it was compounded by having nurses in our home and so many out-of-town hospital stays, plus the extra financial stress. I was shocked at first because I believed what the greeting card said.

It is not some extraordinarily special people who survive the trauma. It is those everyday regular people who humbly draw on the special strength provided by God when their own resources are depleted.

One of the saddest facts in our world today is that marriages are so chaotic, at least a large portion of them. Therefore, many children in Paul's condition grow up either with one parent or in a foster-home situation. That statistic just broke my heart.

When we left Berean, Rudy was counseled by Dr. Jerry Falwell (whom he considered his pastor) and a few other men he respected greatly.

Dr. Falwell told him, "You probably need to get a job because of the financial demands on your family. You're good enough to make a lot more money and provide better that way."

One man in Roanoke, an older gentleman who appreciated Rudy's ministry, offered him a fabulous job with an insurance company. It would include a great salary, a car, and a credit card for expenses. He said that Rudy would have enough residual income within five years that he wouldn't have to worry about money again. This was partly due to a new retirement program for pastors that Rudy helped them design, as an advisor with no compensation.

Those men who counseled him to get a "regular job" were giving heart-felt advice from life experiences. But our conviction from Scripture was that God had called both of us "without repentance" and God does not withdraw or change His mind about those to whom He sends His call. We knew ministry was where we should be.

When I surrendered to full-time Christian service at age 16, I had no idea where it would take me. However, when Rudy asked me to marry him, I knew in my heart that my call was to be a minister's wife. He was called to preach as a young college student and did not feel that had changed. We still feel that way today about our lives' work.

Rudy resigned on Sunday, June 11, 1988, and was in New Jersey the next Sunday preaching in another church.

Many of the men who really loved him helped us a great deal in those days. So many people had called us over the years and asked if we could come and speak, but Rudy was a very dedicated pastor and would rarely miss a Sunday at our church.

We felt that the Lord was now giving us this time to go out and share our story with people who needed it.

As a young couple we had thought we would have a normal family of healthy children, and we would stay at the same church we had founded in Virginia. Rarely, we found, does life follow the path we envision in our youth.

Life many times is like a tapestry that looks beautiful from the front, yet when you look at the back, it looks quite chaotic. You realize only the Lord's hand could produce a masterpiece from the chaos of our lives.

Coming from the family background I came from, I thought that if I married a man with a heart for God and we had a Christian family, it would be perfect.

So many Christians, especially if they had a rough life in the past, think that once they get saved it will be easy. Especially in ministry, people think that pastors and their families are in some way exempt, as if they don't have to pay their bills, have sick kids, or deal with everyday problems. That is so false, but somehow this idea is perpetuated.

Now people see our family and think, "If God has brought them through all these difficult circumstances and allowed them to keep their family intact and stay in ministry, He can bring us through our heart-breaking situation."

The first few months on the road were especially rough for both of us. Rudy had never been away very much from me or the kids. Many times he felt so burdened as he left the house to go out of town that and by the time he got to the main highway he could barely see the road through his tears.

Paul and I stayed in Roanoke when he was on the road. The time apart was especially difficult for me. Rudy had always been a good sounding board and my best friend, and I knew I could safely share my struggles with him. He always knew my heart.

But so many times when he came home from the road we wouldn't have time to talk because we had to unpack and repack to get ready for his next trip. There was little husband-and-wife time.

When you are going through times like this you have to be able to talk to someone. I missed that tremendously and felt terribly isolated. When we talked by phone (there were no cell phones at the time), I was always thinking about how many minutes we were talking and whether he was on the hotel phone because of the exorbitant rates.

This new life was so different. I really couldn't relate to it; it felt like I was walking in someone else's shoes.

Paul and I went to church, and I had to do everything for him by myself, from loading and unloading the wheelchair and all his supplies to being prepared for a seizure during the service, which happened many times.

Paul talked very slowly and had a limited vocabulary. He functioned on a three-year-old level at best. Because of the constriction in his chest during a seizure, he would usually scream loudly. It was a frightening experience to see and hear.

For the first time in my life I really had to force myself to go to church. I knew that God would minister to my heart if I went, and that was always my prayer because I knew I needed something that only He could provide.

It was an ordeal because everything you do for yourself — take a bath, brush your teeth, get dressed — I had to do for myself and Paul. I had to pack plenty of diapers and all of the supplies he needed.

Then we would get to church and it was like a slap in the face because it wasn't our home church, at least not the church we had known and loved for so long. I went with a friend in our town but I didn't join the church because I knew it was temporary and therefore always felt like an outsider looking in.

It was so hard but I knew God would bless me, and He always did.

For the first six months while Rudy was on the road I couldn't do anything outside of caring for Paul. I was still hurting so badly emotionally, I felt paralyzed. The combined effects of concern for Paul, all the recent life changes, and personal hurts pulled me into a black hole clinical depression. At times when the hurts were overwhelming, I would find myself curled in a fetal position on my bed. In my mind when the record player of negative thoughts seemed to go on forever, I would put a pillow over my head. My hope was the recital of events would just stop! It felt as if a pond of quick sand was pulling me under, and no amount of struggle would free me. I cried out in emotional pain to God for help.

God began to work in a still small way literally in front of my face. Of course, I was in such agony I could not see it. We lived in a condominium complex, and my walks would take me around several buildings. I looked forward to crossing paths with an older godly couple who always took a few minutes to chat. Over the weeks as our friendship grew, I shared some of our life's story with them. I notice he always seemed to understand exactly what I was going through and would discreetly encourage me. They finally shared with me that he was a retired military psychiatrist who was now at a practice in Roanoke. God had put this compassionate godly doctor on my walking path. Our Great Physician knew the emotional pain I suffered and answered my plea for help. For a number of months, this psychiatrist worked with me professionally utilizing medication and talk therapy. He helped me move beyond the past and see a future for our family and myself. I am always amazed at God's dealing in our lives as we turn to him for help. Finally I said, "God, I know you are in this. I've got to trust you to do something new with my life."

I started to think about what I had always wanted to do. I had gone from so many outside responsibilities to almost nothing: no social responsibilities, no Sunday school teaching, no deaf ministry, nothing.

We all have a moment where we have to say, "It is what it is. God has allowed this to happen and it's 100 times worse than I thought it would be, but I've got to move forward. I've got to try. Lord, if you will show me one step at a time what to do, I'll do it."

I had wanted for years to be a nurse, even as a kid. Upon high school graduation, my pastor suggested that I go to Tennessee Temple College for one year to get a Bible foundation. I stayed at Temple and ended up marrying Rudy and going in a completely different direction.

Now I was in a unique situation where my nursing education was possible. So I registered for college courses shortly after Rudy started traveling in evangelism.

We could not afford a secretary during this time, so while going to school and taking care of Paul, I also put together a newsletter for our friends and supporters.

We very much wanted the people who supported us in evangelism to know us and not just feel like they were sending their money off somewhere without accountability. Every month the four of us would write something related to what was happening in our individual lives. That "local church" part of us still wanted to be connected to the people who were partnering with us. We told them where Rudy had been and where he was going, so they could be a part of all that was happening in our ministry. We shared stories of how our life's work in evangelism and encouragement was affecting others.

So many times I would fall back on the lessons in the message Rudy was preaching. In ministering to others you often minister to yourself as well.

It took God's grace to trust other people to take care of Paul, and we were in fact trusting God to bring the right people into our lives to help us.

I found myself back to former days when I was in college as far as having to pray in every dollar. We prayed that we could pay Angie's school bill so she could take her exams, and we knew God would do it because He had done it for me. She had never known that kind of need, although I had grown up with it in a large, poor family.

I started to see God's purpose in this new ministry as we were able to reach so many people across the country with our story. In his travels, Rudy ministered a lot to pastors about what they were going through. As he brought back reports from the road I began to feel more validation about what part I was playing in this ministry and that God was truly in it.

Finally I saw that I was going to be able to start my nursing education and get my degree. Also, I could now write a book about our family's life experiences. Rudy had asked me to do this for years. I was apprehensive about this project but felt our story would be an encouragement to others. I prayed to the Holy Spirit, "If You will help me write this book, I'll do it." That was when the healing started, and I learned to trust God anew.

I was able to find meaning in my life again. I had always thought I would be a local church pastor's wife; I didn't think I would do anything else. I must admit, I still longed for our former life; yet God was moving me forward. I was taking classes, writing our book and meeting other people. Also, my phone conversations with Rudy were so important. I wanted to share in his new ministry. The stories he shared were so important. In the summer we were able to travel with him and that interaction in ministry was good for our whole family as we had always worked as a team.

My life as I had known it was over. Angie and Melanie were in other states in college, and Rudy was in evangelism. When Rudy was on the road the loneliness was excruciating for me. A lot of the pain stemmed from the isolation, being at home and away from what I knew and loved. Yet I knew I had to keep my focus on the Lord and not on current circumstances. Even though I did not know the end of where we were going, I did not doubt our Lord had a good plan as He promised. Therefore, we could have hope, which I desperately needed at the time!

We didn't know how we were going to get the original book published. God met our need at a most unlikely time and in a most unlikely fashion.

Rudy had an invitation to speak to 35-40 students at a small Bible college on a very rainy and cold Wednesday morning. A godly pastor invited him to speak at his church that night and give the "Five Lessons" sermon, but he said, "There will probably be only 25 or 30 people there."

After speaking at the college in the morning, Rudy had nowhere to go. Home was three hours away which meant he was stuck where he was. He longed to come home as he parked his car in a local shopping center to while away the afternoon.

"Lord, I know I told You I would never say never, whether it was a group of ten or ten thousand," he prayed in between sleeping in the car, doing some reading and just waiting for the time to pass until the evening service.

As the pastor had predicted, there were 30 or 35 people. Needless to say, Rudy's expectations were not very high.

At the end of the service a man came forward and told Rudy the story of his wife's tragic death due to a wrong prescription after a surgical procedure. He received a large financial settlement because of this, and he had set aside a portion of the money, above and beyond his tithe, to give to people who needed it for ministry.

The man asked Rudy how much he needed to complete the book, and Rudy said he needed three thousand dollars. "I would like to take care of that," the gentleman said.

Rudy was very grateful and said that he would like to tell the pastor first since he was always sensitive, as an evangelist, of any appearance of taking money away from a local church. The three of them met later. The pastor was so gracious. "Absolutely," he said. "In fact, you can give it directly to him or through our church."

That precious godly man gave it to the church, and the church sent us a check. Within a few days we were able to call the publisher and have our book completed.

I think God saw our efforts to be obedient and surrender to Him, and He honored those efforts. God's provision for us to get the book published was such an encouragement to me. I knew God had Rudy in the exact place he needed to be for Him to bless us.

We're all human. Who wants to be out on a cold and rainy Wednesday night under these circumstances? But Rudy went, and to me it was God's confirmation that we were doing just what we needed to be doing.

So many times Rudy went to a church and God moved in such a unique way.

At one church the chairman of the deacon board had just seen his son killed tragically a few days earlier. The church family was turned upside down with anguish at the loss.

"I know you weren't supposed to teach Sunday school," the pastor said to Rudy when he arrived. "But can you just meet with these people?"

He did, and God blessed. Whenever people learned about our circumstances and Rudy was completely transparent, he was able to be a blessing to these hurting people. It wasn't that we had any answers no one else had. It was just that we could relate to people who were in pain because we were in the trenches with them.

Squire Parsons wrote a song many years ago titled "He's Been There, Too" which has a very comforting message. In that song he was talking about the Lord understanding hurt. Rudy, Angie, or I never claimed to have suffered more than others have suffered. It's just a lot easier to understand someone's pain when you've been there, too.

I could tell you story after story of God putting us in positions, where from our life experiences, we could encourage others.

Rudy was at a church in Clark, New Jersey, when a lady came in the back door.

"I can't believe she's here," said the pastor. "This is the first time she's darkened the door of the church since her daughter was killed in an auto accident."

The pastor said she blamed God for her daughter's death and didn't have any use for Him. Nonetheless, she sat there and listened to Rudy's message on "Five Lessons" just as cold as you can imagine. Nothing seemed to move her.

As she left Rudy told her he wanted to give her a copy of our book. She took it, thanked him and left.

A short time later the pastor called and said that she was back in church, and that the book had turned her around. We were so thankful God had used our story to touch this heartbroken lady. Praise to His holy name.

Rudy was in a revival in California when he got a phone call from one of his board members at that time, a Liberty University faculty member named Dennis Fields.

"I just got off the phone with one of our former students, Dave Hirschman, who started a church in Maryland," said Dennis. "He has cancer and is very ill. I wonder if you could just call him. He's thinking about leaving the ministry and just giving up due to his health."

Dave was a former banker with a wife and two children. He got saved and gave up his career to go back to Bible College and start a church.

Rudy talked to him on the phone and told him some of our story. He had already heard a little bit. They prayed over the phone and Dave asked if Rudy would come speak for him when he was back on the East coast.

When he came to his church on a Wednesday night, Dave told Rudy, "You'll never know what that phone call meant to me," He had actually been throwing up in the bathroom when Rudy's call came. That's how sick he was. But after their phone conversation he told his wife he wasn't going to resign the church yet. He would wait a while.

Rudy preached for him and spent the night in the Hirschman's home, sharing our testimony about how God had given grace to us over the years. Dave stayed at that church and Rudy spoke for him again as the years went by.

Dave's church was meeting in a house. Although they had a piece of property, they couldn't build on it. Another church in the area was going bankrupt and about to close. Those two churches merged, and Dave stayed at that church until just a few years ago. Rudy did a revival for him several years after their first meeting.

In 2009 Rudy was walking down the hall at Liberty University's seminary and saw a sign on a door that read, "Dave Hirschman." He hadn't heard from him in years and wondered if it was the same man.

After walking into the office and calling Dave's name, Rudy was embraced like a long-lost brother. They sat down and talked for a while. Dave was finishing his doctoral work with plans to become a professor at Liberty. He is cancer-free now and doing well.

This is just another story of how God used our situation to touch someone else's life.

When we went into evangelism, Dr. Jerry Falwell told Rudy, "If you can preach in 28 different churches your first year, you will be the most successful first-year evangelist I've ever heard of."

We decided to give it a year. At the end of the first year we took a Sunday off around July 4 and went to see Rudy's mom and attend Thomas Road Baptist Church. Dr. Falwell recognized him and had him come up to pray, and then asked to see him after the service.

The board of directors for our evangelistic association was made up of some Liberty faculty members and a few businessmen. Those were the people we were accountable to. Dr. Falwell was constantly asking them, "How is Rudy doing?"

That day we were at his church he said, "I understand you've been doing pretty well. How many churches did you preach in this past year?"

It was hard for us to believe, but the answer was 66. That was, I believe, a confirmation for us that God was in what we were doing.

The second year was equal to the first. There was never a Sunday morning, Sunday night or Wednesday night that Rudy did not have a place to preach.

Our faithful God was leading me step by step into this "new thing" He had for me. I found myself immersed in challenging classes, endless hours of homework, reports, and nursing care plans. My nursing course requirements included clinical practice at the hospital where we could learn the hands-on skills needed to care for patients. In addition, I continued to work on our book, run the ministry office and care for Paul single-handedly for 16 hours a day through the week and 24 hours a day on the weekend.

I thank God that He put so many positive things in my life so there was little time to dwell on discouragement. To be honest, when I was overly tired or lonely, Satan would make me wish for former days. Yet here I was pursuing my nursing degree, walking alongside other people striving to improve their lives through advanced education.

Even without my realizing it, joy began to fill my soul again. No, I wasn't totally in my comfort zone, but I knew I was exactly where God wanted me. As I had stepped out in faith, the Lord put me in a situation where I was able to witness for Him almost on a daily basis.

Angie and Melanie were both in college earning their degrees. Angie was working part-time and ministering at a local orphanage. She lived close enough to us to make the six-hour trip each way to Roanoke, Virginia. Many weekends she came home to help me care for Paul. Angie adored Paul, and she brought both of us so much joy as she would play games or put together puzzles with him. Many times I would hear them laughing together as she would read his favorite books.

Love never fails.

CHAPTER 16
Stepping Out in Faith Again

Rudy spent almost three years on the road, and they were rewarding years. His schedule was full, and he was able to be a blessing to many people.

I had adjusted to our new life in Roanoke as well. Having finished our book, I was able to increase my course load at college. Paul was still going to school and had some outside care.

Angie transferred from Tennessee Temple to Clearwater Christian College in Florida because she wanted to teach special-needs children in public schools. She needed to graduate from an appropriately accredited school to do that.

As Paul was about to turn 21 years of age, we were facing a new hurdle. He would no longer have the option of going to school and the amount of federally-funded care we qualified for would drop dramatically. I would literally be Paul's sole around-the-clock caretaker when Rudy was on the road.

God used these circumstances to lead us back to the pastorate. Rudy felt like he had to be able to assist in caring for Paul. I thought we had gotten some rhythm and stability back in our lives. I thought God's plan was for Rudy to be an evangelist and for me to get my nursing degree.

In early 1992 Rudy came home and told me that he had accepted the pastorate of Calvary Baptist Church in Uniontown, Pennsylvania. My heart sank. I thought, "How can we do this?" Relocating to another state meant all new doctors and not one person who was familiar with Paul's needs. I had told him when I married him that I would be a pastor's wife and go wherever he went. However, the last three years had been very difficult and now everything was going to change again.

Rudy began his ministry there on Easter Sunday but Paul and I didn't move there until the middle of May when school was over. Rudy and Paul drove up in our larger vehicle while I followed in a separate car, crying the entire way. I had just completed my finals, helped Rudy pack our belongings and cared for Paul. In my extreme fatigue and anxiety, Satan had a field day.

"Lord, I just don't understand this," I prayed. "We've been through so much."

I had worked hard toward a nursing degree and now it seemed in Pennsylvania I would not get into another program for two or three years. I was confused about why God would let me start working toward my education and not let me complete my studies.

We were leaving our hometown, our friends, and the people I had learned to trust to care for Paul. Even when Rudy was on the road, I knew I had people in Roanoke I could call on who would be there if I needed them in an emergency.

In Uniontown we settled in a small house, much smaller than the condo we had been in. We did not have any money for a down payment on a home. In fact I thought we'd never be able to own another home because we had gone through personal bankruptcy. Rudy had pledged our home equity and savings on loans for our former church.

Sometimes when you think you've gone through everything and it's over, you find out that you have to go through something new that you never saw on the horizon.

On the Sunday night we arrived in Uniontown, I noticed that a group of our ladies was absent and asked where they were.

"They're down at Waynesburg College," someone answered. "Two of our young women are getting their BSN degrees today."

My heart skipped a couple of beats. "Where is Waynesburg College?" I asked.

"Waynesburg College is about 30 minutes from here," someone replied.

"Oh, they have a nursing program?"

"Yes, they do."

I had been on track for my RN degree and felt all was lost when we agreed to move. I had checked at several universities, from Penn State to the University of West Virginia, and couldn't find an open slot to resume my studies. I had never heard of Waynesburg College, a small, private Presbyterian college just down the road.

I called the dean of the nursing program the next day and went to see her that week. By the following Tuesday I had been accepted and was in a nursing program that would allow me to earn a four-year BSN degree. In Virginia I was in a program to earn an associate degree in nursing. During my tears on the way to Uniontown, God knew He had chosen a bigger and better plan for me. There was a blessing on the horizon; I just could not see it with human eyes.

Within two years, I graduated and was chosen as the Outstanding Adult Student at Waynesburg College. I was able to give God all the glory for being able to go to such a wonderful Christian college and for enabling me to be a shining light to my classmates and professors.

We were able to have a very effective ministry in Uniontown. The people in the church were really good to us and showered us with love.

There was a group of strong, godly men in the church. The previous pastor had faced some problems, and Rudy inherited a few of those. As their leader, Rudy felt comfortable tackling the problems with these men as his confidants and prayer partners.

The church was in some financial trouble, and Rudy was able to make some tough decisions to help the situation because we had been through the fire at Berean as far as finances were concerned. In fact, we were very upfront about our own financial situation when we got there.

Their response was: "Well, you've been through all the things you're not supposed to do, and we will just be the benefactors of that experience."

The congregation numbered 300 to 350 with no Christian school and a very small day care. Because the church was smaller and had far fewer auxiliary ministries, Rudy was able to spend more time at home caring for Paul, especially when I was going to school. Rudy and I would alternate getting up with Paul during the night if he called out for us or had a seizure. If we had a few difficult nights in a row, we would feel like we were in a mental fog from sleep deprivation. After many years of overseeing multiple ministries and then being on the road, it was a great opportunity for Rudy to redirect his energies toward our family.

We had some great people from our church who would sit with Paul; some we paid by the hour and some who donated their time to help us. But it was mostly Rudy's responsibility during this time to oversee his care while I was at school. As soon as I got home, I would study and look after Paul while Rudy handled his ministerial duties.

The church at Uniontown also allowed Rudy to get back into much more of a pastoral, Bible-teaching role. The congregation loved expositional preaching, and he did more in-depth study and preparation than he ever had time to do at our previous church. That got him back in the Word and into better study habits, and it was really therapeutic for him. God's promises and praises brought much-needed healing and encouragement to him on a personal level.

He had a small staff, and the ministry was at a place where it wasn't a catastrophe if Rudy wasn't there early each morning. The pressures just weren't as demanding there, and it was a good place for him to transition back into the pastorate.

The leaders of the church told us we needed to buy a home. Given our recent bankruptcy, we told them it was impossible.

Several men in the church were also leaders in the community. One was a top businessman and another was perhaps the foremost attorney in town. These men and others went to the bank and told them of our situation. Meanwhile, a house was found that would be good for us, but the original builder had not finished it. Another contractor was hired to complete the house, and the appropriate arrangements were made with the bank so we could buy it. Again God provided more than we could ask or think.

We were able to sell that house for a profit when we left Uniontown. By that time our credit score was back where it needed to be so that we could buy another home.

I wanted to find a place of service at our new church and be able to meet a ministry need there.

I had learned sign language years earlier and worked in the deaf ministry at Berean. A deaf couple came to Calvary and there was no one else in the church who could interpret the services for them. I would have to have help with Paul to be able to do that. Another couple at the church, the Blacks, were really committed to helping us in any way they could. They started a special-needs Sunday school class so Paul could be in Sunday school, and they also sat with him during church services so I could interpret for the deaf couple. We also started a Mothers of Preschoolers program at our church, and I was the teacher for this young mother's Bible study. The outreach into our community was exciting as we covered issues such as marriage and parenting skills.

There was so much emotional healing for our family during those years. They honored Rudy as their pastor and they really wanted to help us because they felt that they were obeying God in doing so. God provided a number of unpredictable things when we needed them, which was like a balm for our souls.

There were two things in particular that were difficult for us at Uniontown.

First, we had 72 cumulative inches of snow in a single winter. Severe weather takes on a whole new dimension when you have a handicapped child. There was one month when Paul and I could not even go to church for three weeks due to the church's icy parking lot.

Second, the amount of sunshine there each year is drastically less than in other parts of the country. There were so many bitter cold and overcast days where we found it difficult to get Paul outside for any activities.

After a few years, Rudy felt he had completed his goal for the church to stabilize its finances. He began to sense God had another calling for him. Yet again it was most definitely the unexpected — not just a move to another state but all the way across the United States.

CHAPTER 17
Years of Change

While in evangelism Rudy was invited to preach in a lot of different churches in California. Each time he would speak at a church that pastor would recommend him to another church. On one particular trip he preached at Napa Valley Baptist Church, about 40 miles north of San Francisco. Some time later the pastor called and shared with Rudy that he was leaving the church and asked if he would consider being a candidate for the pastorate. Rudy told him he would begin to pray about God's will for the church and for direction in this important decision.

About this same time, Rudy and I became concerned about Paul's long-term care. There was very limited care provided for people with special needs through state funding in Pennsylvania. Also, Uniontown was a small town in a rural area about an hour away from any large medical centers. In our research, we had learned that the two states with the best care for special-needs clients at that time were New York and California.

Every time we served a church, Rudy and I really grew to love the people. This was certainly true in Uniontown. I admired these people who loved their church and worked so hard to have really good outreach programs. In everything they undertook there was such a spirit of cooperation and a willingness to work. Rudy loved to preach to this congregation as they loved to hear the Bible taught and would eagerly absorb every word he preached. Of course, that encouraged him to study even more diligently as he was challenged by their love for the Word of God.

Graduation for me with my BSN was about two months away. I had made some really good friends in my graduating class and hoped to work in an intensive care unit at a nearby hospital with some of my classmates.

I knew the church in Napa was still pursuing Rudy to consider coming as their pastor, but I tried to put it in the back of my mind. Then one day Rudy came home and said that he felt the Lord wanted him to candidate at this church. This time his decision would include not just a move from one state to another, but from coast to coast.

After the candidating process was over, the church asked Rudy to come as their pastor. When Rudy's mother learned of his decision, she was extremely upset. She had only flown on a plane one time to come and see Paul in the hospital and vowed to never fly again. She stuck to her word and the whole time we were in California the only time we got to see her was when we came back east to visit her.

As with the move to Uniontown, Rudy went to Napa before Paul and I did. Angie and Rudy both came home for my graduation and gave me a beautiful party. I was so thrilled to be honored by family and our church friends but was especially overjoyed when I walked in our den and saw Iris, Paul's nurse of 13 years, there with her husband, Jesus. I was so touched they had driven all the way from Virginia for my party and to see "their Paul." Their love for our family was such a precious gift from God. A couple of days after the party, reality set in as the movers came to pack our belongings. Again, I could feel a sense of sadness and loss at leaving these precious people. I knew God had a new calling for us, but at that moment the familiar felt much more comforting.

The day Paul and I flew to California was extremely difficult. What was to be a five-hour flight turned into a twelve-hour ordeal due to mechanical trouble with the plane. I had packed some snacks for Paul and me but was afraid to eat any myself as the delays grew longer. Also, each time Paul had to urinate, I would have to maneuver him down the narrow aisle and crowd into the bathroom with him. We would try to navigate there before he had an accident in his pants. After a few hours my head was pounding from hunger and anxiety about when we would finally arrive in San Francisco. Due to the delays, Rudy was in a meeting and could not come to pick us up.

Three of the ladies from the church volunteered to come and get us. They were so kind to us in every way. But as we drove through the streets of San Francisco it began to rain and at that moment I could feel my tears trying to spill over. I turned my face toward the window hoping they would not sense my sadness and anxiety. I realized I was extremely tired, hungry, and concerned for Paul, but the task of finding a home, adjusting to a new church and city, finding trustworthy caregivers, and quality programming for Paul seemed daunting. Wisely they just kept talking as if nothing unusual was happening. By the time we found a drive-through restaurant in a rough looking part of San Francisco and I got us something to eat, the terrible urge to cry finally subsided. I thank God that He promises many times in the Psalms that when we are overwhelmed and faint, he will be our refuge, shelter, and strong tower.

I had only been to Napa once before we moved. Rudy had worked hard trying to find us a suitable home. Real estate in Napa cost about twice the amount of a comparable home in Uniontown. The biggest shock for me was how close the homes were to the road and to our neighbors on either side. We soon realized you would have to be wealthy to purchase a substantial amount of land in Napa as it was so highly valued for grape vineyards.

As always, God had a plan for our lives and we were able to find some wonderful caregivers for Paul. The day programs in the state were excellent, even allowing the clients to go on field trips. We were also part of a pilot program where the funding for care was directed by the family. That made more dollars available for families to purchase services as there were no agencies involved.

I passed my RN exams and secured a job working with deaf adolescents in a psychiatric hospital. I felt like I was able to minister to these kids from some really horrible backgrounds by showing them God's love in my care for them. I loved working with these special-needs teens, but my job required me to work second shift which made things more difficult at home. Rudy and I still had to get up many times during the night to care for Paul or just to check on him. There were times we were so sleep-deprived we felt like walking zombies. I can remember having to pinch myself or splash cold water on my face to stay awake.

When a job in administration came open, I applied for it never thinking I would be selected. The Lord provided this wonderful management position for me. It included health and safety teaching, managing the hospital's hazardous waste program, worker's compensation program and the hospital's fitness center. I felt like I was learning so much with all my new responsibilities.

The climate in Napa was wonderful with mostly bright sunny days and mild temperatures. Usually it would rain only between October and April, but then it stopped for the summer. You don't have to worry about your outdoor events being rained out. People are outside all the time, riding their bikes or skateboards, hiking in the mountains, or going to the coast.

Rudy and I loved all the outdoor activities, especially when the hot-air balloons would land in a field right across from our house. We would take Paul up to our second floor on Saturday morning, and would wave at the people in the balloons as they would descend right next to that window. We had a wonderful Christian nurse who worked on Saturday. This allowed Rudy and me to do activities as a couple, something we had not been able to do for a long time. We even took a couple of day trips to the Sierra Nevada Mountains.

Frighteningly, though, one day after Paul had a dental procedure with anesthesia he choked and ended up with aspiration pneumonia. He was in the hospital for about six weeks; many times his oxygen saturation would drop extremely low. We were so afraid this would be the incident that took his life. During this time, he also lost his ability to swallow and a feeding tube had to be inserted.

Paul was such a beautiful child and as we would watch him sleep peacefully or struggle to swallow our hearts would almost break. At times like this from fear for our sweet son, we would feel so helpless and hopeless. Again, through the tears, I would wonder, "Why, God? Why?" You see, it never gets easier. We just had to renew our faith that God knows all and has a plan even for the most difficult circumstances of our lives. Two verses that encouraged me were Psalms 71:1, "*IN THEE, O Lord, do I put my trust: let me never be put to confusion,*" and Psalms 71:5, "*For thou art my hope, O Lord God: thou art my trust from my youth.*"

Paul's pneumonia finally cleared, and we brought him home with the feeding tube. We worked with Paul for months again to train him to swallow. Our efforts were rewarded on the day we found he had accidentally pulled out his feeding tube. By this time he could again swallow enough food to sustain him.

The hospital stays were not only emotionally draining but physically taxing as well. Someone would stay all night as he could not call for help if needed. Many times we would be awake almost all night caring for him and then have to work all day. We never left him in the hospital without one of us there to be sure all his needs were met.

I soon found my place of ministry at the church assisting with the deaf ministry and teaching a ladies Bible study. We found pastoring in California to be quite an adjustment. Living and working so far outside the Bible Belt was a culture shock for us. It was the first area we had ever been in where most people were so nonchalant about the things of God. As a whole, they were not against God so much as they were just apathetic about spiritual matters.

A pastor in the area told Rudy that Napa is in a triangle-shaped area between three mountains. "There is a large concentration of satanic worship within that triangle," he said. "The level of satanic oppression in ministry will be greater here than anything you've ever experienced. You will have a much clearer understanding of spiritual warfare after you live here."

Rudy got another viewpoint from a very godly woman who was a member of our church. "Pastor, you will find here that for most Californians, going to church is just another recreational activity," she said. "If it's fun, you go. If not, you don't. Commitment to church is just not there."

Looking back, it is obvious we were in a different world, spiritually speaking.

After the difficulties at Berean and the heartache of our personal financial losses, after the years on the road traveling as an evangelist, and after working in Uniontown to stabilize that church ministry and its financial problems, some of the toughest years of Rudy's ministry were the years at Napa.

There were so many issues we were not made aware of before we moved across the country. About six weeks after we arrived, the previous pastor's wife, who still attended the church, shared with us that they were getting a divorce. One of their sons was the music director and another son was a leader in the AWANA program. We knew this situation could be very divisive for the congregation, and we were deeply concerned.

Also, just before we arrived Napa Valley Baptist had merged with another church at least on paper. Many times the two groups sat on opposite sides of the sanctuary, making church unity seem impossible. There were good people on each side, but Satan made sure offense was taken by someone almost every Sunday. On church matters, there was definitely a strong undercurrent of opposing opinions on most issues. We had never confronted circumstances like these in our previous churches.

All of the legal and emotional concerns with two congregations that had just merged, plus the previous pastor's family in the midst of a divorce while still attending the church, made for a difficult start. We wanted to support their family during this difficult time, but it proved an emotional roller coaster for our congregation and our family.

Napa Valley Baptist had a brand-new building. Rudy was told the church's debt was under control and there was money in savings. After we were there for a few months, Rudy realized that they did not have any savings and that there were bills that had not been paid. Also, the pastor of the church that had merged with Napa Valley Baptist was threatening to sue the church over retirement money he felt had been promised to him. Please, God, no more surprises!

Rudy spent four years just trying to stabilize the church and get to some level of church unity. He fought every battle imaginable. Dealing with all of the difficulties in the church seemed all consuming. However, Rudy and the church leaders spent much time in meetings and on their knees seeking God's direction in all these problem areas. Psalms 9:10b promises, *"for thou, Lord, hast not forsaken them that seek thee."* They knew their answers rested in God's leading.

Our heart's desire was to be focused on leading people to Christ, discipling new Christians, and starting a recovery ministry for addiction. Yet much of Rudy's time was spent handling problems within the church.

Angie had graduated from Clearwater Christian College in Florida in May of 1993. That fall she taught a classroom of children who had such serious behavioral problems that they were unable to function in a regular school setting. She loved her students and the school where she taught. Both of her roommates got married and even though she was happy teaching in Florida, she decided to come to California.

Due to the cost of living, she opted to live with us. We were thrilled since she had lived far away from us for over six years. With her expertise, she secured a teaching position in Alameda, California, teaching children with behavioral issues. She taught a combination class of boys from grades 5-12. Her students thrived under her leadership, and Rudy and I were so proud of her.

In March of 1995, Angie met Steve Donohoe while working out at a gym where he was training for a bodybuilding competition. As she and her workout partner walked in she saw this mammoth-sized man. He was lifting huge dumbbells and making terrible grunting noises. When he caught her eye she said, "Wow, those look heavy." Joking with her, he replied that in a few months she would be lifting weights that heavy as well. Certainly a stretch, since she only weighed about 100 pounds soaking wet. He introduced himself to Angie. He was so huge, but to her his presence was very gentle.

It was pouring rain that night as Angie left the gym. She heard a knock on the car window. Cautiously, after she cracked her window, Steve slid in a business card. On the card was his name, phone number, and an invitation to breakfast, dinner or just coffee. He asked Angie to call him. Of course, she just took the card and drove off.

Many weeks later Angie again ran into Steve at the gym, and he asked why she had not called. She told him she had no intention of calling him, because for all she knew he could be an axe murderer. He laughed, and as she was leaving the gym asked if he could call her. She tried to convince him it would be a waste of his time as she was sure they had nothing in common. Trying to scare him off, she said, "I'm a pastor's kid, I don't drink or smoke, and I am basically boring."

He did not fall for it and was persistent until she gave him her phone number. Before she would agree to go out with Steve she had some homework for him. First, he had to read my book, *Grace Thus Far*. Second, he had to spend time with our family. Third, he had to promise to come to church with her.

As he read my book, he realized I was the Health and Safety Officer at the hospital where he worked. He told Angie, "I know your mom. At the hospital she is known as 'the church lady.'"

Steve came over on Saturday evening to spend some time with our family before they went out to eat. Paul was the love of Angie's life and the first test every potential date had to pass was how well they interacted with Paul. Steve had no idea what Angie's expectations were, but after he introduced himself to us he immediately went and sat beside Paul on the floor. Steve was completely comfortable and readily interacted with him. His tenderness toward Paul really warmed Angie's heart.

On their date during dinner, they discussed their very diverse backgrounds. Angie told Steve, "My relationship with God and my family are the two most important things in my life. I love teaching and care deeply for my students, but God and my family come first."

Steve, on the other hand, was clearly not a Christian and described to Angie a very dysfunctional upbringing. Although he was not a Christian,

Angie found he was tender and receptive as she talked about her relationship with the Lord. He shared with Angie that he had recently been through a divorce and was looking for something; he just did not know what.

Just as he promised, Steve came to church the next morning. It was evident God was tugging at Steve's heart throughout the services. At the invitation he stepped out and asked Christ into his heart. Immediately he started to read his Bible and attend church faithfully. Steve began to grow spiritually and his excitement about his newfound faith was evident to everyone who knew him. Angie and Steve continued to go out periodically just as friends.

Weeks turned into months, and we saw Angie and Steve start to get more serious. She found him to be funny and easygoing, and he enjoyed participating in our family activities. Steve was very bright and could talk on almost any subject. Yet he had a gentle spirit and always treated Angie with kindness and respect as he did our whole family. He was a hard guy not to like, but there were "red flags" for Angie. We had trained her to choose her husband with great care. Steve had been married before and had a daughter. While we liked Steve as a person and greatly admired his tender care-giving qualities, we were concerned. Steve was nine years older than Angie and had a previous marriage. He had just recently become a Christian, and we weren't sure he understood Angie's commitment to love and serve the Lord.

We knew she would be brokenhearted if the man she married was not passionate about his relationship with Christ. Rudy became so concerned that he talked openly with Angie, and she decided to break things off with Steve. She stated that more than anything, she wanted her dad to be proud of the decisions she was making as a Christian young lady. Rudy and Angie had a wonderful relationship; he has always been very loving and supportive in any endeavor in her life. She knew any concerns he expressed were out of his deep love for her. Angie later stated, "I just couldn't bear the thought that I was breaking my parents' heart."

A week or so after Angie broke up with Steve, she told her dad that even though it did not make sense she knew without a doubt that God had given her peace to pursue a relationship with Steve. Out of our love and admiration for the godly young lady Angie was, Rudy expressed his need to talk with Steve alone. They talked for over an hour, and Rudy went to Angie's room after Steve left to tell her he would respect whatever decision she made. He knew she would listen closely to God's leading in her life. She spent more time in prayer and felt peace about seeing Steve again.

Steve's was one of those lives gloriously changed after his salvation. As he continued to grow in the Lord, we gave our blessing for them to be married. It was very evident to us that Steve adored Angie as he does to this day. We were blessed as we saw God's grace work such a miraculous transformation in Steve's life.

Steve and Angie married July 27, 1996, at Napa Valley Baptist Church. Angie looked like a princess surrounded by loved ones and friends. My sister, Barbara, pushed Paul down the aisle in his wheelchair so he could serve as their ring bearer. Physically, Steve still looked really big from his bodybuilding, but we knew Christ had also given him a "mammoth heart."

They leased a condo in Napa, and Angie taught in the school system in Vallejo, California. Steve graduated in the spring of 1997 with his degree and passed his exams to become a registered nurse.

We knew God had brought us to Napa to serve Him at Napa Valley Baptist Church. He gave us many opportunities to grow spiritually as we had to trust His leadership for this emerging congregation.

CHAPTER 18
Paul's Home Going

*A*s Rudy became assured he had completed the work God had for him in Napa, he began to investigate where our next place of ministry would be. He was invited to join an evangelistic association. They would provide Rudy an office with the secretarial support and other resources that would be needed. Rudy was considering that and even started thinking about putting together a brochure.

An old friend called and asked if he could put Rudy's name into consideration to pastor a church in the mountains of North Carolina. The chairman of the pulpit committee called, and they had a preliminary chat.

Another pastor in California was looking to move back east, and Rudy recommended him to available churches he knew. Later Rudy got a call on behalf of that pastor from Tom Hamilton, chairman of the pulpit committee at Grace Chapel in Sanford, North Carolina. Mr. Hamilton called because Rudy had been listed as a reference.

The man in question turned out not to be the right fit for the church, which both parties mutually agreed upon. When Mr. Hamilton called that gentleman back and they discussed the situation, the pastor said out of the blue: "The guy who would really fit your church is Rudy Holland."

When Grace Chapel was getting ready to return to the resume pile, Mr. Hamilton had breakfast with Rev. Bob Yandle, who had been pastor of the church years before. He and Rudy had made a trip to the Holy Land together. Mr. Hamilton recounted the phone conversation to Rev. Yandle.

"If you can get Rudy Holland, you ought to get him," said Rev. Yandle. "He's got school experience and you have a school. He is a church builder and the church needs to grow. Plus, he's originally from North Carolina."

When Mr. Hamilton called back and asked about the pastorate at Grace, Rudy initially said he was not interested. Tom called back a few days later.

"I've talked with some other pastors around here, and we'd really like to talk to you," said Mr. Hamilton. Rudy agreed to send a resume.

That same week, he got a call on a Sunday afternoon from Johnny West, head of the pulpit committee of another Baptist church in the Greensboro-High Point area. Rudy said he wasn't sure if he was interested in candidating, but he would pray and think about it and get back to him. Johnny's brother was a high school friend of Rudy's, and Johnny called him after talking to Dr. Jerry Falwell.

When Angie came home, Rudy told her he had three churches in North Carolina expressing an interest in him as pastor in the past two months. She looked at him and said, "Dad, does God have to send you a registered letter?"

He laughed at her comment, but it made him think even more.

In subsequent conservations with Tom Hamilton, Rudy expressed his concerns regarding Paul's care. A woman in the church who was a retired hospital financial administrator called us back after learning that North Carolina now had the same kind of special-needs care guidelines as California, which was incredible news for us.

Rudy preached at a Sunday morning "Friend Day" service for one of his former preacher boys about 90 minutes from Grace, so he stopped by that night to check out the church. The sanctuary was full, with about 400 in attendance, and Rudy was asked if he could meet with the men before the service.

He thought they meant the pulpit committee, but more than 30 men representing every leadership position in the church came to the meeting. They started drilling him with questions and he asked what was going on.

"California is a long way from here," said Tom Hamilton. "We figured we'd find out while you're here if you're interested or if we are. If not we won't have to bring you back to find out."

Rudy was very impressed with Grace, so he agreed to come back and preach in view of a call. He and I agreed not to come unless he got at least 92 percent of the vote. I came with him this time, and after the service we traveled to Connersville, Indiana, for a conference.

We got 98 or 99 percent of the vote, and after going back home we felt impressed of the Lord that we should come to Grace.

Rudy started in Sanford on Easter Sunday in 1998. Paul and I did not relocate until October because our house had not sold. The housing market out there is so volatile; you either make a lot or you don't make anything. We caught it on the downside and that hurt our equity position. When it finally sold, we didn't make what we needed to.

The move was easier this time in part because I knew it was coming, since Rudy had been talking to Grace for a while. I had more time to think about it than before and that made the transition easier.

Paul was more stable the first four years or so in Sanford before he started going downhill physically. God blessed us with some good, godly nurses. Paul still had to have constant care due to his electrolyte imbalances and his numerous grand mal seizures.

Dilantin, an anti-convulsant medication, leeched the calcium from his bones, making them very brittle. When he had a seizure, the pressure could cause a fracture in his back, and over time we could tell it was really uncomfortable even while sitting. The last X-ray we had done showed eight fractures down his spine.

Paul was in and out of the hospital but never for long-term stays. The longest he stayed the last six years of his life was probably three or four days for severe seizures or electrolyte imbalances. We knew there was no more we could do for him. If the tumor came back, there could be no more surgery.

It was a matter of giving him the best quality of life that we could making sure that his every need was met and medicating him to the best of our abilities. Any additional invasive procedures were out of the question because his little body had grown so weak.

He had always been so happy and smiled often. That made us happy because so many special-needs kids just don't have that. We did birthday parties and celebrated every milestone with him. We never treated him any differently than Angie as that was very important to all of our family.

The years spent at Grace have been very good years. Rudy has been instrumental in establishing a child development center for ages 0-4, serving approximately 168 children. Our Christian school now averages approximately 300 students. The church has grown, and we have added evangelistic and medical mission trips for our youth and adults. Each of our Sunday worship services is broadcast numerous times during the week, reaching many who do not attend our church.

There was one interesting setback just after we arrived. Rudy found out that the church had voted before he got there to build a building but never got around to actually building it. They had voted two other times but decided later that the timing was not right to get started.

"We need somebody who will take the bull by the horns and get it done," the church leaders told Rudy.

"I'll get it done," he said.

God allowed us to get it built, but there were other challenges along the way such as a fire that destroyed our sanctuary on October 7, 2003. Our church rose to the occasion, and we set up chairs for all church activities in our gym and then took them down for school. This lasted for four long years until we moved into our beautiful new church and classrooms in October, 2007.

Angie and Steve relocated to North Carolina in December of 1998, just a few months after we did. We had become such a team in the way we cared for Paul.

The most significant event during that time was that they wanted to get pregnant and were not successful. Studies were done and they were told that they had a slim-to-none chance. When they moved, they started working with a fertility clinic at the University of North Carolina.

They had been praying that God would work a miracle. Just before their third visit, Angie did a home test and found out she was pregnant. God proved Himself faithful and gave them the desire of their hearts. What was so significant for Rudy and me was the fact that Paul could never have children, and we knew Angie and Steve were our only hope for grandchildren.

Rylee Catherine Donohoe was born December 16, 1999. Jon Patrick Donohoe arrived November 19, 2001. What a wonderful blessing they are to our family. God is always so good to us.

The day Jon Patrick was born, Rudy went home to pick up something and was going back to the hospital when another car pulled out directly in front of him and jammed the driver's door, pinning him inside.

When he heard the news, Steve jumped in his car and came to the scene of the accident. The EMS was already there trying to get the door open. Rudy was injured and stuck in the car.

Steve started crying and covered his face, saying, "That's the only real daddy I've ever had."

The EMS said they would need to get the "Jaws of Life" to get the car open. Steve said, "I'll get it open." He went over and used those massive arms of his to bend that door enough so that several of them could get it open the rest of the way.

Paul had been doing fairly well in Sanford except for the obvious fact that he was becoming weaker and less functional. He was wearing down mentally and was not as vivacious and talkative. We watched him become quieter and more reserved. Any Sunday that we thought he felt well enough we would take him to church. Yet more and more often he would fall asleep from the fatigue of getting there.

We so appreciated the excellent care we had for Paul in North Caro-lina. Since Paul first became sick as a child, our family had to learn to live with someone in our home most of the time, whether it was a nurse or some other caregiver. It was like having a guest who came and stayed for 25 years. Day after day this situation was very difficult. We never felt complete freedom to talk or just be normal. It's hard to live with someone constantly in your home and to be relaxed with your family.

In 2003, I got a job as a nurse consultant in Chapel Hill that required me to go into the office only one day a week. When we were at Napa I led my hospital department through the Joint Commission process for accreditation; that experience made me a good fit for this position. I was really thankful as I love working in nursing. God was faithful again to give me the desire of my heart.

I was working in Chapel Hill on the Thursday before Easter — April 8, 2004 — when Paul's nurse realized something was wrong and that he needed to be taken to the hospital. She called Rudy. By the time he got home Paul's lips were turning blue, and he was having a difficult time breathing. Angie also came over because she wasn't working that day.

Many times Rudy would pick Paul up in his arms and take him by car to the emergency room, but this time for some reason he chose to call an ambulance.

The EMS personnel came and took him to the hospital. When they got there Rudy called for our family doctor, who is a member of our church. He examined Paul and put him in intensive care so he could be closely monitored.

Rudy called me from the hospital, about a 45-minute drive from Chapel Hill. I drove as fast as I thought even remotely safe. In Napa, Paul had aspiration pneumonia, but we were able to pull him through then with tenacious medical care. Though I wanted to get to Paul as quickly as possible, I had no reason to dream that everything would not play out the same way as before.

When I got to the hospital I went directly to Intensive Care. Paul was doing poorly. His vital signs were not good. However, he rallied a bit later in the day.

We stayed at the hospital all that day. The staff worked diligently to care for Paul. Angie and Steve and many of our friends were there for support. That night when he stabilized, I told my family I would be fine there by myself overnight. Rudy decided to go home, rest for a while and come back the next morning. We instinctively moved into our familiar pattern of trading off so that someone was with Paul at all times.

I called Rudy later and told him, "Paul's vital signs are doing really well now." We were hopeful, as always.

The next morning at about five o'clock, it was as if someone just suddenly woke me up. The nurse wasn't in the room at the time, yet I definitely remember the sense that someone was there. I do not know how to explain it except it just felt like there was a presence in the room with us.

Paul still seemed stable at that moment, but soon the nurse came in and said, "We don't understand it. He looks great, but according to the monitors he's starting to crash."

I remember thinking, "Lord, you're not going to take Paul home now, are you? We've been through the tumor, the cyst rupture, thousands of seizures, multiple illnesses and nearly lost him so many times."

In my spirit, I knew something different was happening. I called Rudy and told him to come quickly. I also called Angie; she always made me promise to call her if anything ever changed with Paul. She said she didn't know why, but she was already up and dressed. She normally did not have to get up that early.

Rudy and Angie were both there shortly before six. I never knew how they found out so quickly, but our family doctor and his wife, who is a nurse, came over also. By this time our worst fear was becoming a reality, all of Paul's vital signs began to drop.

The staff came in and told us he most likely wasn't going to make it. We wanted him to go in peace, so each one of us took the time to tell him how much we loved him and that we were ready for him to go because he had suffered enough. We knew that in Heaven all our prayers would finally be answered, and our precious son would suffer no more. God's promise to us was that one day we would be there with him and see him well and whole again.

One of the sweetest parts about it, to me, was when we all prayed over him. Angie said, "God, You better give him the biggest reception you've given anybody because he's loved you and honored you his whole life."

While we waited our doctor whispered to Rudy, "I think I'll turn the monitors off." His wife stood there with us while he went out into the nurses' station to watch the monitors for Paul's last breath. When that happened, he motioned to Rudy that Paul was gone.

By this time, a little before 7:00 a.m. on Good Friday, many people were there — parishioners, friends and family. Rudy had his arms around Angie and me, and he said, "It's Friday, but Sunday is coming." I was so thankful that Paul died very peacefully and that he did not struggle at the end.

Years before when I worked in an adolescent psych unit, one of our patients was a young girl from Africa who for whatever reasons had been separated from her parents. At night she would wail in agony for her mother. I remember thinking, "How can a human being make such a woeful sound?"

When Paul died I heard somebody wailing, and it took a few moments before I realized it was me. That woeful sound emanated from my anguish to let go of our child. I felt as if a hot searing knife had been plunged into my heart.

Dr. Torgerson came in and told us we could go home. His wife was also there, and they told us they would stay with Paul until the funeral home came. We thanked them for their kindness, but we told them we would like to stay because we had never left Paul alone before. One of us had always been there with him every step of the way.

I remember how Rudy, Angie, and I sobbed and comforted each other while asking ourselves how we could possibly go on without our precious Paul. I guess I went into shock because I don't remember most of the day beyond that.

We had bought a little Sheltie puppy in Napa, and he became Paul's puppy. His name was Baxter. He would detect a change before Paul had a seizure and bark so we would know he was about to have one. He could sense an aura that we could not perceive.

After saying goodbye to Paul, Angie and I left the hospital, while Rudy waited there for the funeral home to arrive. When we came home without Paul, Baxter became unbelievably sick. He was throwing up, in the house and up and down the driveway.

One of the members of our congregation is a veterinarian. Two of the men from our church had to take Baxter to his veterinary hospital. The doctor was able to medicate him to stop the vomiting. It seemed as though Baxter just knew what had happened to Paul.

After he came home from the vet, Baxter became my buddy. He made every step I made as a companion and guard dog until he passed away earlier this year.

Our church was unbelievably kind to us. They came to our home to comfort us, pray with us, and to bring food. They could not have been any more kind and supportive. We thank God for all the sweet Christian people God has placed at Grace Chapel Church.

The two men we chose to conduct the funeral service were Dr. Jerry Falwell and Dr. Dino Pedrone. There was an electrical storm that was so severe Dr. Pedrone could not get out of Miami, therefore, he was not able to attend. Graciously Tim Murr, our dear family friend and Rudy's associate pastor stepped in for him.

The same storm system moved into our area. The pilot of Dr. Falwell's private plane told him on the approach that he couldn't land, and they needed to go back to Lynchburg, Virginia.

"Put it down," Dr. Falwell said. "I won't miss this one."

The pilot said, "OK." He put it down and was right on the money.

Dr. Falwell really showed his love for our whole family. He truly had a pastor's heart, and had always been so supportive of Rudy.

The funeral service was so sweet. Paul's favorite song had always been, "Jesus Loves Me." Tim, Jennifer, and Joel Murr, who are like extended family to us, sang that for him.

I have summarized the eulogy presented by Andy Murr, Paul's childhood best friend:

"I was blessed and honored to become Paul's best friend when I was six years old, and he was five. My family moved to Roanoke, Virginia, in the summer of 1978. My father accepted a position on Dr. Holland's pastoral staff at Berean Baptist Church.

I remember staying with the Holland's the first night I was in town because our parents had gone back to get our belongings. I was a little scared and sad, it was a stormy night and I had just met these people, but Angie and Paul both were very comforting to me. I was excited that they had a boy my age. He was the first boy I met in Virginia, and we quickly became best buddies.

We spent a good deal of time together. We played at school, at church and in each other's homes. We made up games and played all kinds of things.

Paul liked to pretend we were in charge of the church. He would give me a hymn book and have me lead the singing, and then he would preach. His sermon likely had similarities to whatever sermon his daddy preached the previous Sunday. Paul wanted to be a preacher just like his daddy, and I believe he would have been a great preacher.

Nearly every Sunday one of us would try to go over to the other one's house for the afternoon. I remember someone telling me Paul was sick and trying to explain to me how sick he was. I didn't understand what a brain tumor was and Paul didn't look sick. I just wanted my best friend to be OK.

As time went by and his condition worsened, I remember going to his house. He began to have trouble remembering things we had done.

There were ups and downs, and I continually prayed for my friend to get better. The Holland's were gracious and allowed me to continue coming over. One afternoon we had to start wearing name tags so Paul would know who we were.

I asked why this had to happen to someone with so much promise and potential, and why it happened to such a wonderful family. I have so many unanswered questions even twenty-five years later, and while I know God's plan is perfect I will still have to ask Him why when I get to Heaven.

We lost contact with the Holland's as both of our families moved out of Virginia, but I continued to pray for Paul. Sometimes when I got discouraged about my circumstances or began to doubt something God wanted me to do, I would think of Paul. God used him to minister to me during so many defining moments of my life, to motivate and inspire me to serve God more completely and without hesitation or reservation.

When Joel called me and told me Paul had passed away, I was actually reading about Christ's suffering on the cross. I thought about how Paul and Jesus had both suffered but that neither was suffering anymore. Heaven is our home, and I look forward to seeing Jesus Christ return that much more so that I can see my friend again."

Rudy, though visibly broken, spoke sweetly of our family's love for Paul and his passion to preach.

"We went by this morning to say our final goodbyes to our little boy. My wife said to me, "We've known for twenty-five years that this day would come, but when it came it was not any less difficult." It was very hard to say goodbye.

It has not been a burden, but a privilege to take care of our Paul. He was full of laughter, and even after his brain damage he was full of life, and love.

His passion was always the same. Before he was ill, his desire was to be a preacher. He visited bus routes when he was five years old, and he led others to Christ before he was six. He stood on the platform at various churches and shared his testimony of how Jesus came into his life. After he was brain-damaged, his constant burden was to see that people know Jesus Christ. I just hope that I have learned from my little boy a little bit about having a genuine passion.

Angie said something recently that I had never really thought about. "You know, I never looked at Paul as a little brother or a little boy," she said. "He was more like an angel." In a lot of ways, I understand that now.

Rudy struggled to read the following I had written for Paul:

A Mother's Tribute

Most of you today did not have the opportunity to know Paul as we did because he had become much more weakened and disabled with time. So please let me share with you a few glimpses of a truly great human being.

Why God blessed Rudy, myself, Angie, and later Steve to have the honor of seeing such a Christ-centered life in action remains a mystery to me. If I had never even heard of a personal loving God before I knew Paul, his life would have directed me to Christ. You see, as Thomas did in John 14:5, Paul had to ask, *"Lord, how can we know the way?"* Jesus answered, *"I am the Way, and the Truth, and the Life."*

That truth became Paul's guiding light, for when there was no way in a thousand different life experiences, Jesus made a way. And for our family, the best part was that we either got to be the coach or the cheerleader.

Also, over the years, the myriad of caregivers who had to do so many tests and treatments on Paul would wonder how he could remain so positive and sweet. That strength came from Paul believing Jesus was the truth. If His Word stated that He formed us in our mother's womb, loved us, and had a great plan for each of our lives, then that was enough truth for Paul.

This attitude was harder for us to participate in as a family, for we were continually wanting and hoping for a "fix" down here, but that was not God's plan. He wanted to use Paul just as He did, as a preacher of the Gospel in all its dimensions. Here I thank God that Paul got to be my teacher.

Lastly, Jesus said that He was the life. For Paul, I think that was the greatest challenge, for he wanted to live his life like he felt Jesus would. We saw him, in the midst of incredible suffering, reach out to others with love, compassion, and humor to try and make their lives better. From this perspective, Paul was our role model, for he truly understood the first gift of the Holy Spirit — love. Paul utilized this gift and all the others that flow from it.

You saw the Special Olympic medals in Paul's casket today. To me, they represent the child and young man that Paul was. The test of a man's character is what it takes to make him quit and Paul never quit trying; and today he soars like an eagle.

Heaven was so blessed on Friday morning, April 9, 2004, when Paul became part of that team. I know he felt right at home with Jesus: his earthly Way, Truth and Life. Paul's hope has become his reality as our Lord promised.

I want to close by sharing that we, as a family, have loved every day taking care of our precious Paul. There have been days that it took strength way beyond what we had, but God's wonderful grace always sustained us. Our prayer today is that if Paul's Savior and Lord is not your Savior and Lord, you will ask Him to be so today. Your decision would give Paul the greatest joy, for he wanted to be a preacher in life and death.

He is in Heaven today rejoicing in the truths we have shared with you. I am sure he is up there coaching and encouraging you to make your decision for Christ, shouting, "Do it, for you ought to see me now!"

We love you precious Paul, and our greatest joy will be to see you soar in the heavens like an eagle and enjoy the best God has for you and all of us who love Him.

Mom and Family

Angie Holland Donohoe recorded the following to express her love and admiration for her brother:

"Today I am paralyzed with pain as we have had to let you go. Please know that I could not be happier for you, but selfish me just wasn't ready, though; I know you were ready to stop hurting.

You deserve to go; you have fought a long, hard fight. On Friday morning when I realized this would be your last fight, I asked Jesus to give you a grand entrance into Heaven. I gave Him lots of great ideas. I know He is so proud of you, Paul. What a testimony you have been. No one can ever fill your spiritual shoes.

You've preached to thousands, especially to me. One of my greatest memories is of you asking people anywhere, at anytime, "Are you saved?" If they stood in shock or simply shook their head no, you would say, "Then I will pray for you right now." You probably remember leading me to the Lord several times, because when you would ask me if I was saved, I would say no just so you would pray with me. Those memories are so precious.

You know all of those sermons of Dad's you were planning to steal? Well, you did great writing your own. Many a night I would wake up and hear you in your room talking. I would peek in and see you sitting in your bed, looking at yourself in the mirror, just preaching away. I hope in Heaven you get to reminisce with Jesus about all the great times we had as a family here on earth.

I could go on forever, but I had better close. You know I will be talking to you frequently. You couldn't keep me quiet here, and you're certainly not going to keep me quiet there. You were my little hero, and I feel so privileged to have been Paul Holland's sister.

You left this world hearing me say, "I love you, Paul." You know, I was always a little bossy, so if you don't mind, when I enter Heaven I want you to be standing there all by yourself, big and strong, beside Jesus to greet me.

I love you, little man."

The following is a poem written and read by Tim Murr:

He's Been There

I can feel the sorrow and, of course, I surely do,
And I can say the usual lines and quote some verses too.
But I can't say that I know all the things you're going through.
For I can't say with honesty, "I've been there just like you."

I can send some flowers and a lovely card as well.
And I can say, "I'm here for you" and other comforts tell,
But I can't really share the pain that you are going through.
For I can't say with truthful lips, "I've been there just like you."

But there is One who's been there and He knows the way you feel.
He has the power to comfort and for broken hearts to heal.
No I can't truly understand what all you're going through.
But He can say, "It's all right son, I've been there, just like you!"

Hebrews 4:14-16

I wanted to share with you some of the intimate and personal tributes written and said about Paul for two reasons. First, we wanted you to sense how deeply our family loved our "special" son. Second, we all need to acknowledge a truth even more important in the light of eternity. It does not matter if you are a child, or feel yourself an insignificant person; God can use your life in a most profound way.

At times Paul had full communication, limited communication, or almost no communication, yet his love for God and others was never concealed. You may think that impossible, but Zechariah 4:6b states, *"Not by might, nor by power, but by my spirit, saith the LORD of hosts."* So our prayer is that God will do great and wondrous things through our lives and yours. These blessings come, as you can see, not from great personal ability or talent but as the Holy Spirit flows through a surrendered heart and an available life.

It was lightning so hard at the end of the funeral service that none of us could go out to the grave site. The funeral home officials feared it would not be safe for anyone around the tent due to the severe electrical storm.

The following Sunday, one week after Easter, we were leaving the gym after the morning service when our doctor met us at the door.

"Pastor, I've got to tell you this," he said. "When Paul died, a couple of nurses came to me and said, 'Did you feel what we felt?'"

He began to cry as he acknowledged that he felt it also.

"I've read and heard stories about this but I've never experienced it," he continued. "As Paul was going, it felt like we were all being lifted."

"Pastor, the angels came for him. It was obvious."

We heard from people all over the country, some of whom we hadn't heard from in years.

I told my sister I hoped no one would be insensitive enough to suggest that we were relieved. We never felt that way. Paul was not a burden. He was our son, and it was our joy to be his parents. Yes it was difficult, almost physically and emotionally overpowering at times, but as Philippians 4:13 promised, *"I can do all things through Christ which strengtheneth me."*

Of course, there were times of questioning. I wondered why God would allow Paul to be born to suffer so much. The verse God gave me at this time was I Corinthians 2:9. *"But as it is written, Eye hath not seen, nor ear heard, neither have entered into the heart of man, the things which God hath prepared for them that love him."* I knew God had wondrous blessings prepared for Paul because he had loved God so much, even in sickness and suffering.

It is one thing to think about Heaven in general terms with a sense of wonder. It's quite another matter to think about it when your own child is there. You have such a sense of urgency to know what life is like in the presence of God. I asked for comfort as I devoured books about Heaven. I wanted to know everything I could.

We had always prayed for Paul to be healed, even when we knew it would take a miracle. I finally grasped he was healed; it just had not happened here. On nights when I could focus on no more seizures, fractures, back pain, or wheelchairs for Paul, the tears would flow a little less frequently.

I found it takes a long time to even begin to get over the death of a child. For most people, it feels like your heart has been ripped in two. You lose the desire to do anything. It is part of the depression associated with such a loss. You wonder why anything matters or, "What's the point?" The agony of missing Paul permeated to our bones. At times the sorrow in our home was almost palpable. One such night I read John 11 which relates the sickness and death of Jesus' dear friend Lazarus, brother of Martha and Mary. Jesus loved these friends dearly but when He heard the news of Lazarus' illness, He waited two days before He started for their home. "Why?" Because He knew these events were timed that He might be glorified as the Son of God. As you read the remainder of the story, it reveals Jesus knew He was going to raise Lazarus from the dead. Yet when Jesus was met by Martha and then Mary who was crying, verse 35 states, *"Jesus wept."* Jesus was troubled in his spirit and wept with the loved ones of Lazarus in their time of sorrow. He understood the pain of earthly death for the ones left behind in grief. What comfort these thoughts brought my broken heart. Jesus' heart is touched with our grief; He cares deeply for us in our deep dark agony of loss.

I think it's important for people to understand that no one can tell another person how to grieve. Rudy and I love each other dearly, but we don't approach most things the same way. I think the demands of work were probably good for him. Someone said one day that it didn't look like he was as affected, but that wasn't even remotely true. I think grief is just expressed in many different ways.

I know it was painful for our families and friends to watch us grieve so. Everyone wanted to help, but no one could fix our emotional pain. Only the Lord could accomplish that, and it would take time.

I do not pretend to understand everything that happens. I do know we live in a sin-cursed world, not just because of Adam and Eve's sin but because of our own sin as well. But the "hallelujah" side of it is that, as Christians, we will one day fully understand the "why" as we grasp God's complete plan for our lives.

Years ago people were more likely to give spiritual platitudes such as, "God has a purpose in this" or "All things work together …" Now most people understand, especially in the early stages of grief, it is better just to say, "I'm really sorry for your loss. If there's anything I can do for you, please let me know." Sometimes you can just send a card saying, "I love you and am praying for you."

I didn't want to become bitter, even though there were moments of bitterness. The pain eventually becomes less acute though it never leaves. From our personal experiences, we wanted to encourage other hurting people helping them with the tragedy in their own personal lives.

Our desire was for Paul's headstone to represent his life as much as possible. Most of the people in our community really didn't know him well because by the time we got to Sanford, Paul did not go out as often. He didn't talk very much and could not interact with other people so they did not get to know the funny and sweet boy he really was.

We put a lot of time and prayer into what the information would reveal about Paul. Steve wrote the following for Paul:

HOLLAND

"PAUL, THE PREACHER"

Heaven's angels are rejoicing

For lost souls you helped to reach

God allowed you earthly suffering

For crowns you joyfully reap.

There is a musical note and the song title, "Jesus Loves Me" because he loved music. When he was so deathly sick and would be vomiting and in pain, we would sing that song to him. Also on the headstone is the reference John 3:16, his favorite Bible verse.

Nearly everyone I've talked to has referenced difficulty in changing such things as the bedroom of a loved one who has passed away.

The last time Paul went to the hospital was by ambulance, leaving behind the wheelchair that took him everywhere. It sat in his room for a couple of months. Finally Angie said, "Mom, you probably should give someone Paul's wheelchair. I don't think he will need it again."

I had not even changed the sheets. Nothing had been touched. It took about three months before I could change anything. It was two years before we finally moved out the hospital bed and put in bunk beds for our grandchildren.

Disassembling your loved one's special place seems to be a common difficulty. It's something that people have to do when they are ready. No one can be rushed through their grieving, and these steps are part of the healing process.

I think in the beginning you need those personal items to hold on to. People need to understand that those physical reminders are comforting due to their attachment to your loved one.

We have pictures of Paul all around our home. We made the decision to always talk about Paul as he is part of our family.

Psalm 23:4 states, *"Yea, though I walk through the valley of the shadow of death, I will fear no evil: for thou art with me, thy rod and thy staff they comfort me."* Many times when Rudy would read this passage to a grieving family at a funeral, I would feel fear in my soul. I would sit there and think, "Will I be able to trust God in the valley of Paul's death, or will I crumble in despair?" In spite of my faith, I did not feel confident I could hold myself together to bury my child. Yet God is always faithful and is able to do more than we can ask or think. For truly in our "shadow of death" experience, my Lord was with me, His rod and His staff did comfort me. The Lord was my shepherd who restored my soul.

As the months passed, I praised God that He had preserved me. I struggled mightily, but my faithful shepherd did not let me crumble in despair. Like Job after he lost his livestock, his servants, and his beloved children, I too grieved through the illness and death of Paul. Yet because of our blessed hope in Christ, I could cry out in the night, "The Lord giveth, and the Lord hath taken away."

Honestly, I felt our time of deep dark testings had come to pass. However, our adversary, Satan, was in the wings waiting to smite us again. Just as Satan smote Job physically with loathsome and painful sores from the sole of his feet to the crown of his head, he attacked us emotionally to the core of our being through our son-in-law, Steve. Remember, *"We wrestle not against flesh and blood, but against principalities and powers"* (Ephesians 6:12).

CHAPTER 19

Drug Addiction—
Surely Not in the Pastor's Family

When our son-in-law, Steve, became so seriously ill less than a year after Paul died, it was like we were totally blind-sided. I thought we had "passed the test," spiritually, by making it through our ordeal with Paul. Suddenly we were thrown into the throes of Steve's illness, and trying to help Angie care for him and Rylee and Jon Patrick, our grandchildren.

I think it's significant to let people know that when you think you are at your lowest point, disaster can hit again. Sometimes that is even harder because your reserves are mostly depleted. We certainly felt that way.

The real questioning came then as we wondered why God would allow this illness after what we had just come through for the past 25 years. My perception was that our time of testing was over, but it certainly was not.

I will now try to take you through our family's journey of Steve's devastating illness and subsequent prescription drug addiction. On a link from our website, Steve has been willing to record his own story. He shares from his heart how he fell into this web of Satan to deal with the physical and emotional pain of his undiagnosed disease. My story reflects how Angie, Rudy, and I tried to care for Steve and the children and carry out our other responsibilities for over five horrendous years. God gave us the grace to get through this nightmare, but sin has consequences and leaves scars.

As you read this part of the story, I hope you get a sense of the insidious cycle that a saved, vibrant Christian can fall into. Satan is duping so many in our society today with prescription drug abuse. People become addicted to these "legal" drugs and the devastation to the addict and his or her loved ones is astronomical. However dark and fearsome our journey became, God never left us or forsook us. As Angie, Rudy, and I trusted the Lord, He gave us the strength to care for Steve and the children and for Rudy to continue to pastor. Also, when Steve finally returned to his love for the Lord and his family, victory came for him also. He is actively working through a 12-step recovery program and is participating in the Christian recovery program at our church. God has opened the door for many others to admit and seek help for addiction after Steve's public testimony at our church.

Our story reflects the eternal truth of Romans 8:28. Certainly not all things, including addiction, are good; however, God can use all things together for our good. Steve is now clean, and he and Angie are using his addiction to walk alongside others and encourage them to break free. Thank God, He can take the devastating circumstances in our lives and make us better. Yes, we can become bitter, or we can decide to use what we have gone through to help others in like circumstances.

Steve became ill in December of 2004. He had drenching sweats, flu-like symptoms, fatigue, flushing, extreme abdominal pain from constant spells of diarrhea, and vomiting as often as 20 times per day. He lost 50 pounds in six months as the disease rapidly progressed.

In January of 2005 Steve's dad died suddenly from a pulmonary embolism. When he returned from the funeral, we talked about that when a parent dies in a dysfunctional situation it theoretically kills your hopes for ever having a" normal family." In his case, Steve's dream was for his parents to be a part of his life and for his father to be a grandfather to his children. Now that his father had died, Steve suffered the loss of that dream as well.

After Steve came back from his dad's funeral, his symptoms continued to worsen. He was referred to the Center for Digestive Diseases where he was told he had Crohn's disease.

He received treatment there until October of 2005. All the time he was losing additional weight and having all the same painful symptoms. Also, he began experiencing shortness of breath, extreme fatigue, migraines, and insomnia.

After months of aggressive treatment for Crohn's disease, Steve's condition actually worsened. His doctor referred him to the Cary Cancer Center where he was to see an oncologist. The oncologist reviewed Steve's medical records and referred him to a specialist at the University of North Carolina at Chapel Hill. After a completely new workup they determined Steve did not have Crohn's disease, yet his condition continued to defy diagnosis. As Steve could do less and less of his normal activities, we became frightened for his life.

I think Angie did what she had seen us do so many times and tried to focus on the challenges of the moment with the Lord's help. She would search the Internet endlessly for answers, desperate to find anything that could help him. Meanwhile, Angie was trying to work and to take care of Steve as well as three-year-old Jon Patrick and five-year-old Rylee. We helped in every way we could think of while I worked as a nurse consultant and Rudy continued to pastor.

The most amazing thing to me is that God enabled Rudy to stay in the ministry and enabled us to help Angie so soon after the devastation of Paul's death. Most people had no idea how Angie grieved the loss of her brother. God also gave her as a young wife and mother the ability to take care of her husband, to keep working and to care for her children. Sometimes I would just look at her and wonder how she did it.

I think she had seen how God gives you the strength to do what you need to do. She had lived through it as a child with us. Her life verse as a child had been Philippians 4:13 — *"I can do all things through Christ which strengtheneth me."* We saw her cling to that verse as an adult during Steve's decline. He was in and out of the hospital many times and still she kept the children on a normal schedule for school, homework, church, and play.

Steve's health continued to worsen through the fall and winter of 2005. He passed out at work one day in February of 2006, and was transported by ambulance from Raleigh to Chapel Hill. Still we received no answers. Steve was so weak he was absent from work often and stressed about the burden this put on his fellow workers.

Angie remembered the word "carcinoid" from the discharge meeting at UNC and began doing research on the Internet to see if that might sound like what was wrong with Steve. Eventually she found that his symptoms could suggest the presence of a carcinoid or some other type of neuro-endocrine tumor.

A carcinoid tumor can be microscopic in size. People can have them for years while they go undetected. These neuro-endocrine tumors secrete hormones in the body and that causes the multiple symptoms in patients.

Angie found that the number-one researcher in this field was a doctor at Mt. Sinai Hospital in New York, and that his wife headed up a foundation for people with carcinoid tumors. Angie contacted her by e-mail and asked if there was any way her husband could see Steve. She sent pictures and information about his condition, and miraculously, the doctor said he would see him.

Later that month Angie and Steve took their first trip to New York to see this new specialist. They learned he was called the Sherlock Holmes of medicine. His reputation was that he would search tenaciously to find a diagnosis for the very ill patients referred to him. After a complete history and assessment, he ordered a radioactive octreotide scan which shows where the tumor cells are located in the body. The scan did not pinpoint any specific location, but his illness strongly indicated tumor activity. Again they left the hospital with no definitive diagnosis; however, the specialist decided to treat per his symptoms.

Steve gave himself three Sandostatin injections a day in his stomach hoping for improvement. The doctor assured them that the tumor would eventually rear its ugly head and the scan would locate it. Meanwhile, a new test to detect the presence of neuro-endocrine tumors was to be available later that year. Steve's name would be put on the list for this new Carbon-11 PET scan. They felt a ray of hope finally.

The Sandostatin injections helped with the diarrhea initially, and Steve temporarily had fewer hospital admissions for IV rehydration.

Also, financial pressure began to come from all sides. Angie had not taught school since coming to North Carolina. After Rylee and Jon Patrick were born she got her real estate license. She wanted a flexible schedule so either she or Steve would be home with the children most of the time. Angie was now unable to spend as much time on her real estate business due to Steve's frequent local hospital admissions. Steve was incapacitated much of the time and unable to work. Now they had to go to New York for multiple hospital stays.

Although Angie tried to keep from us how dire their financial situation truly was, she finally felt she needed to confide in her Dad. She wanted to ask his advice on how to work through these financial problems. As God is always faithful, He was at work in the lives of some of our church members. Jeff and Karen Reid, Pat Strickland, and Allan Strickland put together a community wide benefit to help raise money to offset some of the medical cost Steve and Angie were incurring. We were so touched at the outpouring of love and participation from so many in our church and community.

At this time in our lives, the oppression of Satan became so strong it almost felt like we could sense it pressing in stronger and stronger on us. One day as pressures mounted, Rudy and I met for a quick lunch. Our purpose was to discuss a game plan to help financially. I knew Rudy had partnered in a car lot with another gentleman the previous year, but we had not received any return from our investment. Even before Steve's illness, Rudy had become increasingly concerned over our personal financial needs as neither of us had any retirement benefits except the small amount we would receive from Social Security. This predicament certainly was not from a laissez-faire attitude as stewards of our money. The realities were because of caring for Paul and moving for the ministry, I did not have the tenure required for retirement benefits from the hospital where I had worked. Rudy had served in independent churches with no retirement package provided. Most significantly, it had taken everything we could make working day and night just to provide for our family and to pay Paul's staggering medical bills.

Rudy and I sat through our lunch and analyzed our financial situation. Both of us threw out ideas of different ways we might help Steve and Angie during this most difficult time in their lives. We prayed for guidance before we left the restaurant. He and I knew God was our source and would provide as He had done for 25 years during Paul's illness.

About ten minutes after we left, my phone rang. The caller ID indicated it was from Rudy. I wondered what he had forgotten to tell me since I had just seen him.

"Hello?"

"Is this Reverend Holland's wife?"

I was confused and alarmed. "Yes. Why do you have my husband's phone?"

The nice man identified himself and told me Rudy had been in a car wreck, was injured, and had demolished his car. I remember thinking this can't be real. I just left him.

While going full speed, Rudy had rear-ended a car that was stopped to make a left turn. To this day, he has no idea why he did not stop. Was the sun in his eyes or was he so stressed that it did not register in his mind to apply the brakes?

I got to the scene of the accident just before EMS personnel transported them to the hospital. Miraculously, neither Rudy nor the other man was fatally injured. Rudy had multiple contusions, lacerations, and a broken foot that went undiagnosed. At this point, out of four adults, we had two down and two walking. Rudy worked from home by phone temporarily and hobbled back to work in a couple of weeks.

In July of 2006, Steve was allowed as the 11th person on the list to have the new Carbon 11 PET Scan. Its purpose was to isolate activity of a neuro-endocrine tumor. This time he was at New York Presbyterian, the only U.S. site for the scan. The test indicated tumor activity in the pancreas. A possible Whipple procedure for removal of part of the pancreas was discussed. This particular surgery is very complicated and brings on a myriad of other problems. All treatment options were discussed.

In early August 2006, Steve was in the ICU at our local hospital with diarrhea and vomiting which his doctors struggled to get stopped. His oxygen levels were low. The local doctors talked numerous times with the specialist at Mt. Sinai. He agreed as soon as Steve was stabilized enough to fly to New York that they would admit him. Mt. Sinai is one of the best hospitals in the world, and while there Steve was evaluated by 13 departments. They had numerous multi-disciplinary conferences and finally Steve had a six-hour exploratory surgery. The plan had been to locate the tumor cells and, if indicated, to perform the Whipple procedure with partial removal of the pancreas. However, visually the surgeon could not locate the neuro-endocrine tumor cells; and felt she could not proceed with such a drastically invasive procedure.

During this particular hospital visit, it was time for the kids to start back to school. The separation anxiety and worry over her dad greatly affected Rylee. On one occasion Rudy went to New York so Angie could come home and spend some time with the kids. Rylee became anxious and fearful. Rudy or I would take the kids to school and pick them up each day and assist with their homework. We did everything possible to keep everything normal for them. Our Christian school also was gracious enough to allow me to sit in the hallway each morning where she could see me. I sat there until I could tell she had relaxed enough for me to leave.

At the time Steve and Angie came home from Mt. Sinai, where the doctors had not been successful in locating and removing the tumor cells, Steve stated he became totally hopeless. To him all the hospital stays had just been journeys down different rabbit trails. Everyone acknowledged he was desperately ill, but no one could tell him what was wrong. It was like he was dying in front of our eyes and there was nothing anyone could do about it.

Steve tried to return to work in November but ended up back in the hospital in early December of 2006. He lost his job December 8 due to having too many absences from work. We saw Steve take a behavioral and spiritual nose dive. His moods would swing at the drop of a hat. Angie felt the hardest oppression on Sunday when Steve became openly defiant with her about going to church. In his tormented mind, going to church and finding God had only brought him trouble. He began to isolate himself from us and to show symptoms of paranoia. He resented his illness and everyone around him.

Steve was a really big strong guy and when he became agitated, I would feel my old familiar emotions of fear and dread from my child-hood creep up. Secretly, I had to push down my fears of overpowering strength and possible violence on the part of a loved one. In the back of my mind, Satan began to whisper, "You or someone you love could get hurt." In this familiar pit of fear, I subconsciously went into my protective mode of watching over my loved ones like a hawk. I felt myself reeling and wondering, "What in the world is happening to Steve?" Angie and I even wondered if the disease process could be affecting Steve's brain.

Clearly Steve's illness had taken a tremendous toll physically, emotion-ally, and spiritually. He had always been a wonderful husband, a very involved and loving father, and a great son-in-law to us. Also, as I shared earlier, he had lovingly helped us care for Paul until he passed away.

Over the next few months, we saw him become more paranoid, resentful, jealous, angry, and finally delusional. We had no idea of the "drug-fed monster" growing inside Steve as he self-medicated his emotional and physical pain. It became obvious that he resented Rudy which made everything much more complicated. We did not know why at the time, but the more we had to help the more incompetent he felt as a husband and father.

In March of 2007, one night Jon Patrick brushed his teeth, forgot to turn off the water, and dropped the hand towel in the sink. Their house flooded overnight while they were asleep, and made it unsafe to live in. The ceilings were falling in on the main floor. Angie and her family moved in with us; they certainly did not have the money to rent anything else while still paying their mortgage.

As hard as we tried to keep Rylee and Jon Patrick from feeling the stress of all that was going on, Rylee must have been deeply affected by what she could sense. Her earlier digestive problems with vomiting, diarrhea, and abdominal pain spiraled out of control. The UNC gastroenterologists felt she needed to go to Cincinnati Children's Hospital in Ohio for further evaluation. On the Friday night before they were to leave for Cincinnati, Steve had to be admitted again to our own local hospital. On Saturday we had to change plans; Rudy and Angie drove to Cincinnati. Rylee had to do a clean out for her colonoscopy on the way which made for an interesting trip. I stayed home to watch over Steve in the hospital and to take care of Jon Patrick. On the following Tuesday, Steve was discharged and flew to Cincinnati to let Rudy return home. Rylee was diagnosed with severe nerve damage to her digestive tract from an earlier virus. She was put on anti-inflammatory drugs which we still give her when she becomes symptomatic. The doctors told Steve and Angie she could have periodic flare ups accompanied by severe abdominal pain for the rest of her life.

During those months Steve was in our home, I observed his erratic behavior. Angie and I both found numerous pills lying around and in his pockets when we did laundry. From my professional experience, I began to suspect that in addition to his undiagnosed illness that Steve might have developed a problem with prescription drugs. After spending many hours in prayer with my face on the floor and tears flowing, I approached Rudy about my fears. To my surprise and hurt, he felt I was overreacting. He most definitely did not feel I should take my concerns to Angie and burden her with anything else. In my heart I was determined to put my fears to rest, yet each day my concerns grew. I continually agonized in prayer over my family. Finally I knew the Holy Spirit had given me freedom to approach Angie.

As I talked with her that day anger flashed in her eyes. For the first time in her life, I could tell she was furious with me. How could I think such a thing about Steve? I assured her through my tears that I knew he was desperately physically ill and emotionally wounded. Yet I pleaded with her as I had with Rudy to acknowledge the erratic behavioral changes we had seen in Steve.

Denial is usually our first coping mechanism, and no one else was ready to acknowledge the "elephant in the living room." At that moment, I was the monster in our family's eyes, not Steve's misuse of prescription drugs. I felt trapped and powerless again in a losing battle as I had years ago as the child of an alcoholic. In their denial, Rudy and Angie apparently subconsciously thought if they did not acknowledge the problem we were facing it would go away. I had no such grand delusion for I had seen my mom try that. We had walked down that dead-end street as we unsuccessfully tried to protect and rescue my dad.

Prayer became my lifeline. I knew there was nothing else I could do at the moment. God would have to intervene, and He proved Himself faithful.

Rudy and I had moved into one of the downstairs bedrooms so Angie and Steve could sleep on our main floor with the children. Late one night, all of a sudden, we were awakened by a loud crash and Angie screamed for me. As we bounded up the steps, she was almost hysterical; Steve was incoherent and lying on the floor. I took his vital signs and his respirations were down to six per minute.

"We've got to get him to the ER," Angie said.

"No," I replied. "We've got to call EMS. His respirations are desperately slow, and he may need emergency medical intervention."

They came quickly, and he was transported by ambulance to UNC. What a traumatic night; Rudy and I grieved as Steve lay unconscious on the bed, and Angie sat beside him tenderly holding his hand. As a family we prayed as we hovered over Steve in that emergency room and pleaded with God for his life.

After a matter of some hours, the doctors came in to talk with us. They reviewed Steve's medications and mentioned methadone.

"He doesn't take methadone," I said. I knew all of his medications — at least I thought I did.

"He is definitely positive for methadone," the doctor replied.

They administered an antagonist for the narcotics to Steve. In a moment he raised up, and his eyes shot wide open. He did not know what had happened or where he was. His response to the antagonist and his labs proved positively that he was using methadone.

After his discharge, he convinced Angie he was just trying to deal with his pain and had taken a few pills he got from a friend. She believed him and was defensive saying that if the doctors had found out what was wrong with Steve and had successfully treated him, he would not have taken the methadone. Angie now admits she was in denial and totally ignorant of the power of addiction at the time.

In June of 2007, the reconstruction on Steve and Angie's house was completed. Steve's erratic behavior continued to escalate, but Angie kept much of it from us. She still felt his illness was his only real problem. Steve's addiction in reality had made him another person who could lie proficiently. He could effectively blame everything that happened on his sickness or someone else's behavior.

Angie called me on July 26, 2007, the day before their tenth wedding anniversary. "Mom," she pleaded, "will you stay up all night if you have to and help me try to figure out what is going on with Steve?" I could tell she felt desperate although she did not elaborate.

I believe so much in the power of prayer. Before I would start my research, I pled before the throne of God for an answer to our dilemma. Methodically, in my mind, I reviewed Steve's history and listed every sign and symptom I was aware of. Noted were euphoria followed by anxiety and sadness, insomnia then profound sleepiness, periods of paranoia, delusional thoughts, and isolation to mention a few. During the long hours of the night I cried out for wisdom as I had during the years of caring for Paul. I drew strength from God's promise in James 1:5, "*If any of you lack wisdom, let him ask of God that giveth to all men liberally, and upbraideth not; and it shall be given him.*"

In the early morning hours, there was no denying we were witnessing the cycle of abuse and withdrawal from drugs. Based on Steve's previous overdose, I suspected methadone in combination with his other pain medications.

Covered in prayer, I approached Rudy when he awoke about questioning the man who had given Steve his methadone pills in April. Rudy said he would support my decision as we knew the man on a personal basis also. I felt at this point we would not get a truthful answer from Steve.

When the man came to our home, I told him truthfully about Angie's call and my research. We pleaded with him to be honest and tell us if Steve was getting methadone and percocet from him. His face registered fear, so we assured him our only purpose was to help Steve. Finally, he told us that Steve had continued using percocet and methadone even after his overdose in April.

I was physically shaking so hard I did not think I would be able to speak as I called Angie. Yet the Holy Spirit empowered me to calmly ask her to come over by herself as we needed to discuss something with her. I am sure she probably thought I had found out some new facts from my research. Sadly I had, but it was not what she wanted to know.

As we talked to Angie that morning, her demeanor dropped. She made one last futile attempt to deny the addiction, but we told her we had already talked to the man Steve was getting the drugs from, and he had confirmed our fears. We cried with her as we told her that we had purchased a drug test kit earlier that morning and asked if she would consider doing a drug test on Steve.

On that morning, their tenth anniversary, Angie pleaded with Steve to tell her the truth about his drug use. She promised to stand by him as he got help. Steve convincingly and angrily denied using methadone and percocet until the moment the test proved positive. Quickly his mood changed to despair.

"I just need to leave," he said. "I'm an unfit husband and father."

Angie calmly talked to him and assured him they would get help for his addiction.

We went to the beach the next week as Tara, Steve's daughter from his previous marriage, was flying in for our annual beach trip. That week was a living nightmare as Steve tried to detox from the narcotics.

We kept the kids busy so hopefully they would not be aware of what was going on. I could sense myself again feeling like I was stuck in a living nightmare from which I could not escape. In the back of my mind professionally, I knew I was sinking into a deep clinical depression. But denial also worked for me, at least temporarily.

After we got back home, Steve was admitted to a 30-day intensive outpatient program at a hospital close to us. To an outsider he did everything he was supposed to do, but we learned soon enough he was only placating us. In his own words, Steve stated, "I had not hit bottom, was still very addicted, and continued to use even during my intensive outpatient program." Until an addict of any kind wants help, you can give him or her all of the help in the world and it won't matter.

Angie called me on her 37th birthday — September 28, 2007.

"Mom, can you come help me?" she said. "Steve's out of control and I'm scared."

As far as Rudy and I knew at that time, Steve had not drunk alcohol for years. But on this date for the first time he mixed alcohol with whatever drugs he was taking, and that made his behavior totally out of control.

We went over to their house because Steve had left angrily and Angie was afraid for his safety. At this point Rudy could not have much to do with him. He had become a thorn in Steve's flesh. All the traits he admired in Rudy when his own life was right now just made him feel incompetent and therefore agitated. Rudy knew he could not physically subdue Steve, but if his daughter and grandchildren were in danger he would not have hesitated to defend them in whatever way he could. At that time Rudy knew it was best to just stay clear of him, if possible.

Later, Steve came back into the house angry and raging. Rudy was upstairs playing with the children so they would not hear and see their father in this kind of shape. Frequently I had seen this kind of behavior years earlier with my own father, and I did not want Rylee and Jon Patrick to have scenes like those imprinted in their minds.

Even with Steve being as big as he was and with his pain tolerance being very high, I remember God gave me such a sense of calm as we faced him. The Holy Spirit empowered us to do what I knew we had to do.

From my earliest memories at three or four years of age, I can vividly remember the violence that came from my dad when he was really drunk. I knew from my own life experience that the most important thing for us was to get the kids out of there safely. I told Angie, "I don't want Rylee and Jon Patrick to see their father like this."

I asked Rudy to take the kids to our house so Angie and I could try to calm Steve down. I knew if we could get him down on the couch he would fall asleep. When he did, I would get his bottle and pour the liquor down the sink. I am sure the Holy Spirit intervened for Rudy agreed to take the children to our house. Angie stood in the foyer as Steve was still very angry with her for calling us and prayed until he fell asleep. However when I poured that alcohol down the sink, it was as if I was having a "déjà vu experience." I was a child again; my dad would fall asleep drunk, and my mom would pour his alcohol down the sink.

Rudy, Angie, and I spent a long night of roller coaster emotions. There was anger at Steve for his behavior, his lies, and the turmoil he was putting his family through. There was also agonizing concern over how we could help him. Angie was deeply worried about Steve's fragile emotional state. He hated where his disease and addiction had taken him, and he was angry with God. Steve did not like the person he had become. Later we found out Angie even feared he might commit suicide. Yet all the love, encouragement, and programs had not helped Steve. We did not know what to do or where to go. During that dark frightening night, our hope and strength came from knowing God promised He would never leave us or forsake us. To the depths of our souls we knew we were in way over our heads. However, we knew we were not alone or abandoned. God would provide an answer as we continued to seek wisdom from Him.

Satan never gives up. That night as I had poured the liquor out of that bottle and down the sink, it felt like my spirit had flowed out of my body along with it. Even though everything turned out all right then, something emotionally had broken for me. All the struggles of my childhood, Paul's illness and death, together with Steve's disease and drug addiction had now made me feel like I had somehow failed everyone I loved.

I became plagued by recurring thoughts that even though I had tried to be a perfect child, that did not rescue my parents. Though Rudy and I searched out and provided the best care we could find for Paul, our efforts had not saved his life. Though we as parents had done everything we knew to protect Angie from any danger, not only she but our grandchildren were in the very place I had vowed my children would never live.

Satan pulled me into a pit of anxiety, black-hole depression, and post-traumatic stress syndrome with horrible recurring nightmares. I was able to hide what was happening to me until my anxiety forced me to resign my ladies' Bible study at church, and I began to scream out for help during my nightmares at night.

Finally, in the spring of 2008, I knew I had to seek help. A wonderful psychologist helped me for months to talk through my pain and to realize I could not have altered any of the circumstances in my life. The medical side of the practice treated me for depression and anxiety. I thank God for these loving and caring professionals. My deep depression finally temporarily lifted.

At present after years of multiple traumas, I still struggle with anxiety, (especially social anxiety and panic attacks), have difficulty sleeping, and wake up with my heart racing and in a cold sweat from frightening nightmares. The toil of witnessing anger and violent arguments in my childhood home, listening even in my sleep for Paul to have a grand mal seizure at any moment for almost 25 years, and waiting for Angie to summon us with a phone call day or night for the next five years with Steve in crisis resulted in my mind constantly anticipating disaster.

For spiritual strength, I immersed myself in God's promises of His loving kindness, grace, mercy, protection, and deliverance for His children. As I drew upon His Word, He strengthened my mind, body, and soul.

As I work through these issues, God has given me a wonderful expanded ministry of personal prayer. God has so tendered my heart for those who struggle. I also volunteer as a nurse for the Helping Hands Clinic in our town. The clinic provides medical care and medications for the uninsured in our community. My ministry focus may have had to temporarily change, but my passion to serve the Lord and others burns brightly.

After the incident at their home on her birthday I told Angie, "Something inside Steve has to be driving him to do this." In October 2007 he was referred to a psychiatrist who began handling his medications and diagnosed him as being bipolar. We have no idea if that diagnosis is accurate because he never showed any indications of manic or depressive behavior before his illness and subsequent drug abuse. However, the medication she gave him began to stabilize him.

Steve's behavior improved although he would still have erratic periods. We later found out these were primarily the result of methadone binges. Angie encouraged and worked endlessly to help Steve with his addiction. Now she acknowledges they wrongly thought he could stop using drugs if he just decided to.

By the end of May, 2009, Angie felt her struggle was useless, and she told Steve she and the children would have to move out at the end of the school year in June.

Steve says this was the defining moment for him. He knew he had hit bottom. Though he had tried unsuccessfully before to work a recovery program, he determined he would go to any length to achieve sobriety and save his family.

Once again, Steve began working the 12-step recovery program. He had been able to go back to work by this time as his disease was in remission.

Steve diligently worked his program for 90 days. However, working his program meant attending multiple meetings per day. After the initial 90 days, Steve's attendance at recovery meetings and contact with his sponsor began to drop off. During this time period, he made a faulty decision. Steve felt he was cured and stopped working the recovery process. He not only stopped attending the meetings but also stopped the daily work that is essential to the success of the program. After he made this tactical error, Steve was able to stay clean for only ten months in spite of his love for his family. The monster of addiction was too strong to handle alone.

On April 9, 2010, Steve had a major relapse and was involved in a minor one-car accident. He was charged with driving under the influence. Steve immediately informed his nursing supervisor; and was able to utilize the Family Medical Leave Act and enter rehab.

Steve finally came to the sobering fact that he was suffering from a disease of the mind, body, and spirit. He found he was powerless in the face of addiction. He would have to surrender day by day and allow God to provide strength and healing. This would be a battle he would have to wage daily for the rest of his life. Recovery is a process, not an event.

Steve became addicted to prescription drugs over three years ago. We as a family never really discussed whether to share his story publicly before September 5, 2010. Honestly, we were so busy dealing with his illness and the ramifications of his addiction that we just lived day to day. I'm sure on some level we felt like we had to protect Rylee and Jon Patrick. Maybe we did not feel there was much anyone could do to help beyond prayer.

Steve Horne, the leader of our church's Lighthouse Recovery Ministry, asked Steve to pray about sharing his testimony at church on Recovery Sunday. As they prayed about his response, the Lord revealed to Steve and Angie it was time to come out with the family secret. They knew from current statistics that many churches have families affected by drug and alcohol addiction. By sharing their family's challenge, they hoped others would come forward and seek healing and victory over this stronghold of Satan.

God has miraculously used Angie and Steve's decision to bring his struggles out into the open. God is using them in a mighty way to help others with addiction as they are in turn helped by others. God has again proven His promises true as stated in Romans 8:28, *"that all things work together for good to them that love God, to them who are the called according to his purpose."*

The Mt. Sinai doctors still feel Steve has a type of neuro-endocrine tumor, and that eventually it will get big enough so they can locate it. They will perform surgery at that time. God will give us grace as He always has to see us through.

Steve continues in his 12-step program and in the Christian recovery program at our church. Angie, Rudy and I, and our church family, continue to pray for and support Steve in every way possible.

John 10:10 states, *"The thief* [Satan] *cometh not, but for to steal, and to kill, and to destroy: I* [Jesus] *am come that they might have life, and that they might have it more abundantly."* Satan has struck our family with wave after wave of extreme difficulty and heartache. Yet our "Lord of Hosts" has brought us through victoriously. Each of us has his/her personal battle scars, but God has protected us as a loving Shepherd. As He promised, not only have we come through it all, but we have had abundant (though many times difficult) lives.

I love the old song that starts with, "I love little baby ducks," and continues to list things the singer loves. My version would read, "I love my wonderful family, my friends, and my church. I love date night with Rudy, family times with Angie and Steve and the kids, and books." My song could go on endlessly, but it would always end with, "and I love you, Lord."

As we close, we pray our story will bring hope and encouragement to you in your struggles. Life's tragedies hurt, and we empathize with your heartache and pain.

At this juncture in our lives, Rudy's mom is entering the throes of Alzheimer's disease. Does it hurt? Yes. Do we at times feel hopeless to help? Yes.

Yet as God's children we have great hope in the loving kindness, grace, and mercy of our Lord. Cling to His wonderful promises to be your guide, protector and strength.

Our family looks forward with anticipation to what God will do through Paul Rudolph Holland (PRH) Ministries. Our first endeavor, to provide scholarships for young ministerial students, continues on an annual basis. A medical mission focus, called Introducing Christ Universally (ICU), started in 2009 with trips to Haiti and the Dominican Republic. Pleas for help have already flooded in from other countries.

Short-term evangelistic mission trips will be our focus for 2011. All of this is done first and foremost in response to our Lord's Great Commission. Also, we do it to further the desire of Paul's heart to reach the world with the Gospel.

As we have opened our hearts and home to you through our story, we pray it will serve as a help to you. Our prayer for you is that when you feel your whole world is falling down around you due to circumstances, you will never feel alone. Even when the direction of your life seems out of control, it isn't. Our Savior knows exactly what is happening and will work everything out for His glory and our good as long as we seek His will.

We are not always certain what paths our lives will take, but we certain in the promises of Romans 8:28 — *"And we know that all things work together for good to them that love God, to them who are the called according to his purpose."*

CHAPTER 20
Lessons We Have Learned

Following is the outline of the sermon Rudy has preached countless times across our nation, and some practical insights God has taught us.

"Five Lessons I've Learned From Tragedy"

I.   I've learned of God's unfailing grace. (II Corinthians 12:8)

II. I've learned of God's inexhaustible supply for every need. (Philippians 4:19)

III. I've learned of God's unquestionable purpose. (Romans 8:28)

IV. I've learned of God's unexplainable peace. (Philippians 4:6-7)

V.   I've learned to expect an unpredictable result. (Philippians 1:6)

There were also many practical truths we learned in dealing with Paul's illness:

✦ Practice the admonition of the Scriptures, *"Train up a child in the way he should go."* As parents we never know what valleys our children will go through; give them something to lean on.

✦ Let your life be a strong and consistent testimony so your child will want to know the same Savior as you.

✦ Honor the Scriptures in choosing your mate. *"Be ye not unequally yoked together with unbelievers."* (II Corinthians 6:14)

✦ Cherish your marriage. Always let your mate know you are there in adversity and prosperity, in sickness and in health, and for better or worse.

✦ Have a time each day to teach your children God's Word. Their salvation must be your top priority.

✦ Instill in your children a love for the local church. There they can be taught how to live according to God's plan.

✦ If tragedy strikes, take comfort in the fact that God is in control of every aspect of your life.

✦ Let others minister to your need through companionship and prayers.

✦ As a friend of someone going through a tragedy, **do something to show your concern**. Send emails or a card, make a short phone call, or stop by for a brief visit. People appreciate any show of kindness and interpret your failure to do so as a lack of concern.

✦ Do not recite stories of friends or family who had similar circumstances.

✦ Be extremely careful about offering unsolicited medical advice. To do so may offend the family and make them feel you do not trust their judgment or that of their physicians.

✦ Be aware that each family member will probably handle trauma differently.

✦ Explain to each child according to age and maturity about the tragedy that has affected your family.

✦ The unknown is usually more frightening than reality, so give everyone involved time to ask questions.

✦ In your concern to protect children from pain, be careful that they don't feel left out.

✦ Take time to help others. These acts of kindness will help alleviate your own pain.

✦ Asking "why" is a very normal reaction when we feel that unfair circumstances have come into our lives. Remember, "His ways are not our ways, and His thoughts are above our thoughts."

✦ Making decisions is extremely difficult during a trauma. Seek counsel, pray, and then rest in the assurance that you made the best decision you knew how to make at the moment. Berating yourself later about a particular decision is self-defeating.

✦ Be aware that the misbehavior of a sibling may indicate unresolved problems he or she is experiencing.

✦ Help the siblings understand that you don't love the "sick" child more than you do them. The "sick" child just requires more of your time. Try to integrate the siblings in caring for the "sick" child.

✦ When others want to help you in a time of need, remember that God will bless them for their generosity. This attitude will help ease the embarrassment you may feel when others are doing for you.

✦ The separation of family members, necessary when out-of-town medical facilities are utilized, is extremely difficult for everyone. Call, send a card, email, or visit as often as is feasible to help ease the sense of isolation.

✦ In reaching out to others in need, offer practical help such as food, transportation or housing.

✦ Try to have pleasurable experiences in your life to help balance the heaviness of tragedy.

✦ Reach out to people in similar life circumstances. They understand what you are going through and can be a real source of strength.

✦ It is OK to admit you don't always have the answer. Sometimes all we can say is, "I don't know."

✦ Feeling angry is normal during stressful times. Talk through your feelings with someone. Pent-up anger will always find an unhealthy way to vent itself.

✦ Realize that doctors don't always have all the answers. They are humans just like we are, and medicine is not always an exact science.

✦ Allow yourself to feel the love of God through others as they minister to your needs.

✦ Be strengthened by the prayers of fellow believers.

✦ You are ultimately responsible for your family's health. Ask your physician to explain any medical procedure you don't understand.

✦ Be prepared for your fears and anxieties to seem much bigger during the night. Combat them by quoting Scriptures, talking to your mate, or getting permission to call a friend if needed.

✦ Do not think that other people expect you to be "strong." They understand you are in emotional pain, and it is OK to admit how badly something hurts.

✦ Don't let your marriage fall into that 80 percent divorce category. Communicate with each other about expectations and failures so problems are handled as they come up.

✦ Never lose hope. Where there is life, there is hope.

✦ Seek out any available help. Many times respite care can be provided for the caregivers by agencies in your community.

✦ If rehabilitation is involved, try to let every family member participate in some way.

✦ If the bills are larger than your budget, call to set up payment plans. Most offices will cooperate with you if they know you are doing your best to pay them.

✦ When you as the caregiver start having health problems, adjust your schedule so you can get more rest. Caregiver burnout is a reality; use strategies to help prevent it from overtaking you. Maybe you won't get all of your chores done every day, but you will find the world won't come to an end if that happens.

✦ When you lack wisdom about how to deal with a problem, ask for the wisdom of God. He has promised this in James 1:5.

✦ Be prepared to sometimes take one step forward and two steps backward. Progress requires a lot of patience.

✦ Rejoice over each small accomplishment.

✦ Holidays are emotionally charged times. Try to observe as many of your family traditions as you feel up to. This helps children especially to feel that not everything in their lives has changed.

✦ At the appropriate time, be willing to turn loose of former dreams and aspirations and refocus on new and more realistic goals.

✦ Humor can be a good friend. It can get you through difficult circumstances.

✦ Be willing to listen to your children. You will find occasionally that they have a better perspective on things than we as adults do.

✦ Be aware of the dangers of bitterness. Do not let it take root in your heart. It is like a cancer that will eat away the good in your life.

✦ When your own strength is gone, remember the power we have through the Holy Spirit. Call upon Him.

"Are you saved?" This was the first question Paul would ask when he met a stranger. What did Paul mean by saved? He was simply asking, "Have you asked Jesus to be your Savior so you can know you are going to Heaven?"

The truth is being saved not only holds the promise of Heaven after this life; it also provides help from the Lord as you have seen by our story.

But how are we saved?

1. Admit you are a sinner. (Romans 3:10, 23)

2. Acknowledge His death on the cross as payment for your sin. (Romans 5:8, 6:23)

3. Accept Jesus as your personal Savior by faith. (Romans 10:9, 10, 13)

Simply stated, "If you would like to receive Jesus as your Savior, pray the following prayer from your heart."

"Lord I know I am a sinner. I believe you died on the cross for my sin. Right now I want to confess my sin and receive you as my Savior. Thank you Lord for saving me."

Sign your name _____

Please call, write, or email us if you have accepted Jesus as your Savior or if we can help you in any way.

CONTACT INFORMATION:

PRH Ministries
3310 Wycliff Court
Sanford, NC 27330

Rudy Holland (919) 770-4794

Doris Holland (919) 353-5331

Angie Holland Donohoe (919) 721-0173
(Contact for children affected by illness in family)

Steve Donohoe (919) 721-3976
(Contact for people affected by addiction issues)

Joel Murr, Chairman PRH Ministries (919) 770-6835

Email address: prhministries@yahoo.com

EPILOGUE
BY RUDY HOLLAND

*T*he journey of grace for us really began when God saved me and my wife, and we both went to college at Tennessee Temple.

She had little money. God provided funding for her education through a scholarship and a campus job. I had my life planned. I was going to be a restaurant owner and already had an offer for a position with a chain of restaurants where I would eventually manage several of them. I had agreed to go to Bible College for a year just to learn the Bible, but then God called me to preach.

The journey of grace then took us to the place where we started a church. It was a perfect ministry family. The church grew and was recognized nationally, and we were given all kinds of accolades.

Then one day we learned that our son, Paul, had a brain tumor.

God's grace was sufficient for us through all those days of hospital stays, sickness, and sufferings. God's grace was also sufficient when we had to say goodbye to him as he left us to go to Heaven.

We thought then that we had experienced God's grace and life would continue with His smile upon us, only to wake up six months later with another challenge. This situation would again require His grace, this time different and in many ways greater than any we had ever experienced. The illness of our son-in-law along with the consequences of that illness, and the choices of his life has led us to draw once again upon the grace of God.

Even as we complete this book, we do not know how much grace we will need in the future because we do not know what tomorrow holds. We don't know the hurts, difficulties, and problems we will have to face before Jesus comes or we go to meet Him. But we hope that we can use these experiences and pass them on to touch and help the lives of other people. To do that, after Paul's death we established PRH Ministries (named after Paul Rudolph Holland).

Right now it has three arms. To date the primary emphasis has been the Paul Holland Scholarship for ministerial students, provided to graduating seniors who are going to college to prepare for the ministry. To date we have three men in full-time Christian service who have received the scholarship; one of them received it twice (for college and for seminary). Also, two other young men are still in college pursuing their degrees.

The first recipient is now serving a church in Florida. The second is serving a church in Georgia just outside Chattanooga. The third is now continuing his education in seminary at Liberty University. The fourth has started a church in Tennessee. The fifth young man entered Davis College in the fall of 2010 to study for the ministry.

The funds for these scholarship awards come from the board members of PRH Ministries and other supporters. The board is made up of Doris Holland, Steve and Angie Donohoe, Joel Murr (chairman) and Andy Murr, who was Paul's best friend.

In recent years God has allowed me to get involved in medical missions. We have assembled a group of doctors from various churches and take them to the foreign field.

One of those doctors has closed his practice and is now a full-time missionary in the Dominican Republic with CURE International and is preparing to go to Africa.

Another is expressing an interest in closing his practice and possibly going to Haiti as a missionary, while a third is also considering full-time mission work. Only one of these three men is a member of the church where I am pastor. The others are at different churches in our city.

As a result of these developments, we began a second arm of PRH Ministries called ICU (Introducing Christ Universally). It is a medical-mission organization that has no funding as of now, but as other medical professionals continue to show interest in it we pray that God will use it to take medical missionaries around the world. They will not only bring physical hope and help, but also the Gospel of Jesus Christ to needy people as they work with missionaries and groups in various countries.

The third arm of the ministry, which has just been organized, is Short-Term Missions. Joel Murr, the chairman of PRH Ministries, is very active in short-term missions while also serving as the youth director of our church. He has a real heart for missions.

We have had several churches ask us to help them with short-term missions, and we have been very successful in doing that.

We want to continue doing that through PRH Ministries to ensure that the mission work perpetuates.

All of this we do in honor of Paul and, most importantly, for the glory of God — to fulfill the Great Commission and do what we can to get the Gospel out.

Hopefully this ministry will live far beyond my wife and me if the Lord tarries, as Angie and Steve perpetuate it and our grandchildren eventually pick up the torch and become involved with the assistance of others God may bring into the picture.

All of the proceeds from the sale of this book go to PRH Ministries. Paul always wanted to be a preacher and he served God to the best of his ability during his time of illness.

Through his story and this new ministry, Paul will continue to preach.

Thank you, Heavenly Father, that even in death you gave Paul the desire of his heart to be a preacher through PRH Ministries. Lord, you do *"exceeding abundantly above all that we ask or think"* (Ephesians 3:20).

Angie at age 5
and Paul at age 3

Paul at age 4 is a Ring Bearer
at a church member's wedding

Paul at age 5 tries out
a new kind of wheels

Paul at age 6 sits
at Rudy's office
desk — he wanted
to one day preach
at his Dad's church

Despite Paul's health
condition, he enjoyed
normal children's activities
with the help of a nurse
at his side — here, nurse
Mary Ann Boggs cared for
Paul, age 9, as he attended
AWANA clubs

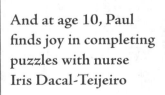

And at age 10, Paul
finds joy in completing
puzzles with nurse
Iris Dacal-Teijeiro

At age 17,
Paul attends
a basketball
game
dedicated
to him

Our family's
1991 prayer card
for evangelism

In 1993, our family attends
Angie's graduation from
Clearwater Christian College

1995, Our first Christmas with Baxter, Paul's companion and guard dog until Paul's passing in 2004

Paul, age 24, and Angie at her wedding on July 27, 1996

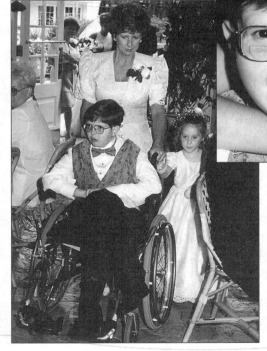

Paul once again serves as a Ring Bearer, this time at his sister's wedding, but rather than walking, he is pushed down the aisle in his wheelchair by his Aunt Barbara

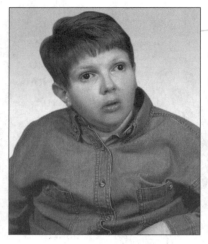

This final photograph of Paul, our precious son, was taken just one month before his home going

In 2001, Rudy with Mom, Ernestine Holland, Angie, and Angie's daughter, Rylee, at 18 months old

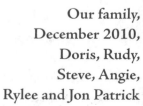

Easter 2004, Rylee and Jon Patrick, Angie's children, look so much like Angie and Paul at the same age

Our family, December 2010, Doris, Rudy, Steve, Angie, Rylee and Jon Patrick